"We all need power to be able to negotiate [...] tive life. The question is whether the pow [...] theologically legitimate or not. In this prop [...] a pressing issue in our time, Fitch criticizes the American church's la-tent cultural Christianity for its ties to ungodly forms of power. A much-needed corrective."

—**Alan Hirsch**, author and founder of
Movement Leaders Collective, Forge Mission
Training Network, and the 5Q Collective

"Fitch has courageously undertaken a long-overdue examination of the relationship between power and the way of Jesus. Fitch asks pro-vocative questions that challenge established paradigms and invites the church to reimagine world change emerging from the practice of radical dependence. *Reckoning with Power* summons readers to a journey of holy unlearning that is the crucial first step to encountering the true, upside-down power of God."

—**Meghan Larissa Good**, pastor; Theology Circle chair
at Jesus Collective; author of *Divine Gravity: Sparking
a Movement to Recover a Better Christian Story*

"As someone who grew up in an immigrant Hmong church, I always felt a power distance between my social location and more enterprising ver-sions of American Christianity. Some evangelicals will have tension—or even disagreement—reading this book because amid the wealth of its sources, it engages with outside perspectives to show how entrenched we can become with worldly power. But I feel some of the tension is appropriate. After all, it is a form of worldly power to be able to avoid feeling uncomfortable and unchallenged in your own church tradition."

—**Daniel Yang**, director, Church Multiplication Institute,
Wheaton College Billy Graham Center

"From that moment in the fourth century when Christians were first offered a seat at Caesar's table, the seductive lure of coercive power has ever been the bane of the church. A return to the dynamic coun-tercultural Christianity that turned the world upside down before the Constantinian catastrophe is possible, but only if we are willing to heed the summons of the Spirit to radically rethink our relationship with worldly power. In response to this summons, Fitch's *Reckoning with Power* is the critical reassessment the church needs—particularly the church in North America. As he writes, 'This cultural moment begs for a reckoning with power.' I could not agree more! I urge those who hope for a better Christianity to read this book."

—**Brian Zahnd**, author of *The Wood between the Worlds*

"At this moment, there's nothing the church needs more than a Jesus-centered theology of power. Without it, the world will rightly turn away. Fitch's book brings that needed word. May the church listen."

—**Beth Felker Jones**, Northern Seminary; author of *Practicing Christian Doctrine*

"Ancient spiritual teachers warned against three great temptations: money, sex, and power. If we understood these temptations rightly and handled them well, many of our maladies would be curtailed. When it comes to power, sadly, too few Christians have bothered to understand or handle it well. Western Christians have fallen victim to the illusion that power is just power and that it is not inherently corrosive in the hands of the 'right people.' Fitch challenges those assumptions by putting power itself under the microscope. No longer will Christians be able to strap on meaningless, empty signifiers, such as 'servant,' to baptize our abusive wielding of worldly power. Fitch asks us to look deeper, question more, and release that which so many of us have striven for: worldly power."

—**Sean Palmer**, author, pastor, speaking and teaching coach

"In a time when American evangelicalism is being held hostage to political and cultural power, Fitch offers another, more kingdom-oriented, way. *Reckoning with Power* should be required reading for Christian leaders and influencers. It is the best Christian introduction to the subject I have read."

—**John Fea**, author of *Believe Me: The Evangelical Road to Donald Trump*; Messiah University

"David Fitch has never been a shrinking violet, instead boldly going after the many idols of our age while pressing toward an account of Christian discipleship that makes the qualifier 'radical' redundant. Here he takes on power using his voice to show how our many accommodations to worldly power go hand-in-hand with accepting power on the world's terms. He calls us instead to Christ's power as the church's first and final reckoning with worldly power. Powerful!"

—**Jonathan Tran**, Baylor University; author of *Asian Americans and the Spirit of Racial Capitalism*

RECKONING WITH POWER

RECKONING WITH POWER

WHY THE CHURCH FAILS WHEN IT'S ON THE WRONG SIDE OF POWER

DAVID E. FITCH

BrazosPress

a division of Baker Publishing Group
Grand Rapids, Michigan

© 2024 by David E. Fitch

Published by Brazos Press
a division of Baker Publishing Group
Grand Rapids, Michigan
www.brazospress.com

Printed in the United States of America

Library of Congress Cataloging-in-Publication Data
Names: Fitch, David E., 1956– author.
Title: Reckoning with power : why the church fails when it's on the wrong side of power / David E. Fitch.
Description: Grand Rapids, Michigan : Brazos Press, a division of Baker Publishing Group, [2024]
Identifiers: LCCN 2023030365 | ISBN 9781587434150 (paperback) | ISBN 9781587436253 (casebound) | ISBN 9781493444908 (ebook)
Subjects: LCSH: Church and the world. | Christianity and culture. | Abuse of administrative power.
Classification: LCC BR115.W6 F58 2024 | DDC 261.7—dc23/eng/20230817
LC record available at https://lccn.loc.gov/2023030365

Baker Publishing Group publications use paper produced from sustainable forestry practices and post-consumer waste whenever possible.

24 25 26 27 28 29 30   7 6 5 4 3 2 1

Dedicated to the staff of Northern Seminary,
both recent past and present.
Thanks for your service to Christ.
May we work together for an organization
free from the abuse of worldly power,
filled with God's holy power,
for God's mission in the world.

CONTENTS

INTRODUCTION

The American Church on the Wrong Side of Power

> Not by might, nor by power, but by my spirit, says the LORD of hosts.
>
> Zechariah 4:6

The standard account of power says there's only one kind of power in the world and we, the good people, must get on the right side of it, using it to bring justice into the world. Power is power. It is the way the world works. There is no getting around it. And so let us get the good people in charge of that power, putting it to work toward righteous ends.

What follows in this book calls that standard account into question. Instead of that account, I intend to show that there are really two kinds of power at work in the world, not one. There is worldly power, which is exerted over persons, and there is godly power, which works relationally with and among persons. Worldly power is coercive. A person or organization takes control of things with worldly power. Worldly power is enforced. It is prone to abuse. God's power, on the other hand, is never coercive. God works by the Holy Spirit, persuades, never overrides a person's agency, convicts, works in relationship. Through His power God heals, reconciles, and reorders not only our personal lives but the social worlds we live in as well. God's power works not just personally in individual souls but also among social realities to disrupt oppressive social systems and bring justice to the world. God's power is miraculous because it always works beyond the expectations of human imagination (Eph. 1:19; 3:20–21).[1]

Seen through this lens, to be on the controlling side of worldly power is to be on the wrong side of power. Cooperating with God's power is the right side. Certainly, there will be times for Christians to use worldly power, but always for limited ends. It is when Christians use the coercive power of the world to do the unlimited work of God in the name of God that they are unequivocally on the wrong side of power. All hell breaks loose, abuse and trauma follow, and we have a dumpster fire on our hands. This book attempts to dissuade all Christians from being on that wrong side of power.

Power and the American Church

Take a quick survey over the landscape of the evangelical church in America and you see the ruins of power gone bad. You see morally failed leaders and sexual abuse perpetrated or excused by pastors. In the name of Christian nationalism, you see Christians seeking political power everywhere to enforce a Christian culture over America. In its wake, you see destructive violence unleashed with self-righteousness. You see ugly racism and misogyny either ignored or defended in the name of God. It is all an unconscionable mess.

As a result, many of us are shaking our heads, disillusioned with a Christianity gone sour. We cannot trust the church anymore. We've been watching a parade of abusive leaders fall, one church at a time, wreaking irreparable damage on our institutions and our witness. Our churches, and their leaders, have become notorious as abusers of power. We want to reject those forms of power, but we still need power. We don't know what to do with power.

It is this cultural moment that begs for a reckoning with power. We need to take an inventory of what has been happening. It's time to move beyond the bandages that seek to hold our institutions together by managing the power better each time we go through an episode of a scandalous leader and institutional disgrace. Instead, let us go deeper to examine the corrupting power that lies beneath it all. Amid our shock at what has become of the American church, let us examine the way power works and how the church is called to live under a different power: on the right side of the power of the One who reigns until all have been made subject (1 Cor. 15:25). This is the invitation of this book.

Why Does This Keep Happening?

In recent years, many books have narrated the history of evangelicalism's abuse of power and the destruction it has wreaked on people's lives. Jemar Tisby's *The Color of Compromise* described the history of evangelicalism's (and its predecessors') complicity with slavery and racism.[2] Anthea Butler's *White Evangelical Racism* accomplished a similar feat.[3] Kristin Kobes Du Mez's *Jesus and John Wayne* detailed the evangelical church's cultivation of a toxic masculinity and patriarchy within its own culture and politics.[4] Kevin Kruse's *One Nation under God* told the story of evangelicalism's (and its immediate predecessors') leaders joining with corporate economic power to gain the control necessary to lead a "Christian nation." John Fea's *Believe Me* outlined the evangelical church journey to align politically with Donald Trump.[5] These are just a few of the books that have been published within this genre in the last decade. They all-expose, in horrific detail, the history of evangelical Christianity's complicity with abusive power that led to hideous cultural sins.

These complicities, once revealed, leave us incredulous, asking, "Why does this keep happening?" Are these examples of just a few bad apples in evangelicalism, or is there something woven deeply within the fabric of evangelicalism itself that leads again and again to these moral failings? Are these examples of Christianity or apostate heresy? Or is naming something apostasy just an easy out? Is there a problem in the design because this same apostasy keeps happening again and again in the name of Christ?

In this book I seek to answer these questions by asserting that it is evangelicalism's (as well as many other past historical Christianities') complicity with worldly power that has led to its present demise. It is the church on the wrong side of worldly power. But just as important, when the evangelical church has been on the right side of God's power, in submission to Christ's power by the Spirit, some of the greatest social revolutions in history came forth.

Unfortunately, evangelicalism (and Protestantism in general) has often failed at discerning the difference between worldly power and godly power, between being on the wrong side of (worldly) power and the right side (of godly power). The modern Christian's understanding of power is thin, and it has fostered a regular alignment with worldly power in the name of Christ, and it is ruining us.

There is no escaping it. The problem of power lies at the core of evangelicalism's failure to be the church, the social body of Christ's power in the world. It explains the church's complicity with grotesque injustice. It is the how and why of a church gone apostate. And so we need a better theology and practice of power. This is the reason for being of this book.

Jesus and Power

In Mark 10:35–45 Jesus's disciples are jockeying for power in the coming kingdom. Given their assumption that the kingdom was imminent as they looked toward Jerusalem, James and John assume power will look like worldly power over people's lives, and they jockey for the seats to the right and the left hand of Jesus, the positions of power. Upon hearing about this, the other disciples get angry, not liking that they are being sidelined in this process. Jesus gathers them together and says these famous words: "You know that among the Gentiles those whom they recognize as their rulers lord it over them, and their great ones are tyrants over them. But it is not so among you; but whoever wishes to become great among you must be your servant, and whoever wishes to be first among you must be slave of all" (vv. 42–44). This episode repeats elsewhere in the Gospels and is played out over and over again in Jesus's ministry. It could not speak more plainly of Jesus's theology of power.

Jesus is saying in no uncertain terms that worldly "power over" shall not be part of His kingdom. Indeed, worldly power closes off the space for God to work in His power. According to Jesus, the use of worldly "power over" is not just a problem for the church of Jesus Christ; it is a heresy for this church, and it impedes the church's calling to be the center of Christ's healing power at work in the world. For those who are in His kingdom, worldly power is not an option. It shall "not be so among you."

And yet among most Protestants, evangelicals and post-evangelicals alike, we are tempted to go the way of power, worldly power, to do God's work. Jesus, we think, is too impractical to get things done. We believe that good people changing laws, and then enforcing them, will change the world. We believe that godly experts, putting into effect new programs from the top down, will change our churches. We believe that the abuse specialists implementing accountability into the leadership structure will keep the leaders in line. We believe that by educating people to be more aware of their racism, patriarchy, misogyny, paternalism, abuse of power, and all other grievous social sins, we can surely induce these people to repent and change. And all these approaches will surely accomplish some changes. But I suggest that, apart from reckoning with the power that undergirds our systems, drives our cultures, and corrupts our leaders, these changes will merely be window dressing, making things look better while the same power with its corrupting tendencies perpetuates itself until the next time it blows up in our faces all over again. These changes will at best be a bandage put over the problem of power, covering over the cancer that metastasizes beneath the surface of our lives.

This book urges us to avoid bandage solutions to this gaping wound of the church, a wound we name as the abuse of power. Instead, let these sins of power be revealed for the sinister forces they are, at work deep beneath the surface of our lives as Christians in the West. The problem, you see, is power. It is not just the wrong use of power. It is being on the side of the wrong power. It is being on the wrong side of power. We need a theology and practice that enables us to see power for what it is and see how it works so we can be on the right side of God's power, under the power of God unleashed in Jesus's person, work, and reign, participants in the power of the Holy Spirit extended from Jesus and at work in us and around us.

What Follows in This Book

What follows in this book is an exploration of the idea of power, how it works, how we think about it, how it shapes the way we lead and otherwise do the things we do in church and in the world. It explores the church's relation to worldly power in the church of evangelicalism but also the modern Protestantism that preceded it in North America. It digs deep into the ways worldly power corrupts human beings and institutions when power is exercised in independence from God. It asks, How can we practice leadership and engage the world differently in the power of the God of Jesus Christ, for His mission? How can we be the people of Jesus under His power?

The story I wish to tell begins in chapter 1 with a multilayered description of what power is. Reviewing the best thinking on power from the past one hundred years, I summarize a consensus of how power is defined today—specifically, worldly power, power that works independently of God. This review, though brief, is important, for it shows the complex ways that power works and provides a backdrop for the skills we will need in order to recognize it working and recognize its corrupting effects around us.

The reader should be aware from the outset that I focus mainly on power in the West. I aim to focus on how we in the West, especially the Euro-Christian tradition, came to understand power and the way it works, and how that understanding made way for so much abuse, pain, and destruction. Even more specifically, I want to expose the way worldly power has poisoned much of what has become evangelicalism within this present Euro-Christian edifice. I will engage some non-Euro voices within the West, because they are essential to any such reckoning. We are all caught up in power's orbit in the West. But it is outside the scope and breadth of this book to draw on the entirety of world Christianity and its many traditions in this survey of power. The goal here is a reckoning with how power has been shaped in the West and how, in turn, it has shaped all of us—no matter what ethnicity, sexuality, or class—who live in its shadow.

Having defined power in chapter 1, in chapter 2 I explore the power of God at work in the world and how that power is so different from worldly power. It is in this chapter that we are confronted with Jesus's pronouncement: "Not so among you." As we journey through Scripture, the distinction between the two kinds of power becomes clearer. I suggest that this distinction is key to navigating being on the right side of power. It is key to cultivating a new faithfulness for the church in our time.

Chapter 3 describes how the two powers have been both distinguished from each other and blurred down through church history in the West. In the history of the church there's a pattern of both seeking to maintain the distinction between worldly power and godly power and then almost irresistibly blurring the two soon thereafter. The church is continually tempted to take up worldly coercive power in the name of God and be on the wrong side of power. Yet each time it happens, things do not end well. But when the church heeds the words of Christ—"Not so among you"—and comes under the power of Christ and His Holy Spirit, the church flourishes in the most unanticipated ways.

This leads me to chapter 4 and a look at evangelicalism itself and how it has fallen into this trap of blurring the powers via current-day "Christian nationalism." I describe how there are surely times when even Christians must participate in worldly power. But there are limits to this power, and if we dare exercise worldly power in the name of God and His purposes, we find ourselves on the wrong side of power. Abuse, trauma, pain, and destruction are sure to follow. There can be no compromise ever for the church itself in the way it lives in relation to power. When we are the church, living in the confines of the social spaces of His church, Jesus commands unequivocally, "Not so among you." If we defy Jesus, taking control of worldly power to do what only God can do through His power, we find ourselves dangerously on the wrong side of power. This place is so dangerous because an institution or person, given worldly power to accomplish basic tasks, starts acting like God and becomes unwieldy and hell-bent on destruction. The true colors of the wrong side of power are revealed.

In chapter 5, I describe three of the more compelling strategies within evangelicalism that tempt us continually to the wrong side of power. In three cases, in alluring fashion, we are tempted to use worldly power for God's purposes: the temptation to use worldly power to do God's justice in the world, the temptation to rehabilitate abusive power in Christian leaders and keep it within guardrails so they can continue to use it for God, and the temptation to "leverage privilege" for kingdom work. These strategies all have some merit as they hope to limit the damages done by worldly power. But if these strategies end up convincing us that we as Christians are the ones who can use worldly power for God's purposes, we too will end up on the wrong side of power all over again. We will stretch worldly power beyond what it can do, leading to eventual abuse and marginalizing God's wonder-working power among us, in our churches, in our neighborhoods, and beyond.

A final chapter reflects on the church today. I ask what it might look like to live under the power of God at work among us. Frankly, we need a new imagination for how "we get things done" without worldly power and the abuse it leaves in its wake. How might we as Christians in the twenty-first-century West live into the kingdom of Jesus? Many churches of the West, in which the habits of Christendom, enlightenment rationality, and secularism are deeply engrained, have no imagination for a church that does not run on worldly power. And so it is important to offer some glimpses of church leadership practices, social justice, discipleship, evangelism, and multiethnic church that renew imagination for a church living in and witnessing to the power and presence of the living Lord.

Before ending the book, I offer an epilogue. It narrates a different story of evangelicalism than the ones Tisby, Butler, Du Mez, Kruse, and Fea tell. These authors, mentioned earlier, all tell the story of the church on the wrong side of power. As a result, these churches have all been on the wrong side of history when it comes to slavery, the oppression of women, poverty, sexuality. Perusing the histories of slavery, oppression of women, and poverty in North America and examining the histories of the churches/leaders that supported and enabled these cultural sins versus the churches/leaders that didn't, I ask, Where did these churches sit in terms of privilege, posture, and worldly power? What side of power were they on? I then notice that whenever the church was among the oppressed, giving up worldly power, making space for godly power in Christ, soon thereafter abolitionist movements, women's suffrage movements, workers' movements, and ministries to overcome poverty ensued. In stunning ways the culture was transformed. Whenever the church aligned with worldly power, it either limited its work for the kingdom or outright compromised that work in the most hideous of ways.

And so as it turns out, whenever the church was on the wrong side of power—that is, aligned itself with worldly power—it ended up on the wrong side of history. But when it heeded the call of Jesus—"Not so among you"—and became present among and with those *not* in worldly power,

God worked, and He worked powerfully to transform the world. And the church cooperated with Him. And so, when it comes to the church's work for God's justice in the world, the question of which side of power the church will occupy moves to the forefront. The church that is on the wrong side of power will inevitably be apostate. The church that lives under the power and presence of God, on the right side of God's power, is unleashed for social revolutionary works of salvation.

On Gender-Inclusive Language for God

One little note before we dive into this journey. Over the years I have struggled much with the well-known problem of using masculine pronouns to refer to God. I deeply sympathize with all women and men who hear patriarchy and abuse every time God is referred to as a "he" or "father." I haven't come to peace with how to rectify this issue, maintain the interpersonal nature of God, and maintain a sense of the history of the tradition, all at the same time. This book argues with no reservation that God and godly power are not coercive, never "power over," always interrelational, never patriarchal. It is because God is interrelational that I need to express God as a person. To speak of God as "he" and "him" or as "she" and "her" does this because gender describes an interrelation. But I wish to do so in a way that disrupts and overcomes patriarchy. It is in this sense that I continue to use masculine pronouns and "Father" for God and Jesus the Son and feminine pronouns to refer to the Holy Spirit (in line with a historical precedent). Yet each time I do, I have chosen to capitalize the terms. By maintaining gender in my language for God I do not mean to say God is actually physically gendered, male and female. I mean to say God is interrelational. In that God created humans as gendered "in God's image" (Gen. 5:1–2), I believe I am highlighting the personal nature of God, that God is in relation, whenever referring to God as "He" or "She" versus another term. It is to affirm God as triune God, interrelational, and creator of creation. I hope all people can give me grace as they read this text, as I am signaling with each capitalized term that I am using these terms in this specialized way. For now, this is my solution, perhaps a temporary one.

I have been careful to disguise the details in the stories I share in this book in order to protect the identities of those involved. I tell these stories from my own place of experiencing them or hearing them being told.

And so let us journey together. Let us explore the history, the Scriptures, the sociology, to discover God's way in navigating power.

1

Defining Power

The Many Versions

> For our struggle is not against enemies of blood and flesh, but against the rulers, against the authorities, against the cosmic powers of this present darkness, against the spiritual forces of evil in the heavenly places.
>
> Ephesians 6:12

Power is everywhere. Even when you don't see it, you still know it's there. You sense it. Its pressure pushes in on you.

Let's imagine a fictional first visit to a Sunday morning church service in Chicago. As you enter the sanctuary, you're approached by a person known as a greeter, who hands you a clipboard and with a smile asks if you'd be comfortable giving the church your personal information. This seems intrusive. You feel uncomfortable. But you oblige.

The greeter then points out to you a pledge on the clipboard that asks you to attend at least four Sundays before you make a decision as to whether to make this your church. The church is already making assumptions about you, and you haven't even sat down yet. After some group singing and worship music, a video appears on the screen up front. It plays a popular television commercial with Matt Damon saying the phrase "fortune favors the brave." The pastor then steps onto the large stage and notes that the video clip is an illustration for today's sermon. He compliments the congregation for their courage amid the COVID pandemic.

He then asks if anyone is depressed, struggling, disobedient, or even lazy in their Christian faith. He declares that Jesus is the deliverer and says this church shall live with courage. He declares that this church, unlike other churches, is here to serve the "down-and-outers." This too will take courage. There's an altar call—a ritual that some churches do— where people come forward to be prayed for. The pastor invites any among the audience who seek courage for their lives to come forward and be prayed for. The church service ends. As you walk out, the greeters smile at you again and thank you for coming.[1]

Power was being exercised in that gathering on that Sunday morning, and pressure was being applied to submit to it. Nonetheless, the power was not easy to discern. No one forced you to attend that church service. No physical violence was wielded against you. But social pressure was evident. You were being seen and categorized. A subtle pressure was being applied to conform to expectations by very nice people with toothy smiles. The sermon addressed you. And if you responded by going forward at the altar call, you were assessed and expected to submit to certain behavior expectations. The pastor had a role in this church and had been given much authority. You'd be submitting to that too. In a sense, in that Sunday gathering, you were being inducted into a whole scripting of power in that church. You sensed it but it was hard to put your finger on.

Power is present in almost all social situations we find ourselves in. Whether it be the corporation you work at, the village zoning committee, the street crew you work on, the neighborhood, the playgrounds, the sports organizations, the local schools, or that charitable organization you volunteer at, power is at work. In all these places persons have stakes in what is going on. Each organization gathers a people for a purpose. And power is what moves us and what gets things done. Power is also at work in your local church.

That being acknowledged, power can work for good or for ill. It can be used to help people live and flourish. It can wreak enormous harm on people's lives. Unleashed, aligned with evil, it can kill sixty million people in a war and destroy entire cities (World War II). Power can abuse, trick and beguile, lie, deceive, restrict, and oppress. To use power in this way is to be on the wrong side of it.

Strangely, this can happen even at a church, through a church, and maybe especially in a church. The church can be on the wrong side of power. And because people trust God, people derivatively trust church and are therefore open to power abusing them in God's name all the more by those in power who wish to use them for their own purposes. Power seems so much more dangerous in a church, and so Christians must not shirk from discerning it. Every church must be equipped to discern power.

The first step in this direction is to define power, then study how it works for the good and how it goes bad. How can we discern bad power from good power? Most of all, we must examine how it works in the church of Jesus Christ. For here is where the wrong side of power should be exposed for what it is.

In recent years we have seen horrific abuses of power by the church, corporately and by individual leaders in the church. If we are to get to the bottom of these massive failures in the church of North America, we must begin by asking what went wrong with the power behind these abuses. To do this we must define power—what it is and how it works. And then we must discern if there is a difference between the way power works in the world and in the church. Let's start by defining power.

Defining Power—Power Over

Power, as most people define it, is that which one person (or system) exercises "over" another person (or system). The key word here is "over." Power has been studied and written about for hundreds of years. From Marsilius of Italy, to Machiavelli, Hobbes, and Nietzsche, the history of the West has been obsessed with it. But we begin most simply with Max Weber, a nineteenth-century sociologist, who described power as "the probability that one actor within a social relationship will be in a position to carry out his own will despite resistance."[2] In political theorist Robert Dahl's words, "A. has power over B. to the extent that he can get B. to do something that B. would not otherwise do."[3] Both writers point to this basic idea of power: it is the exerting of one person's will "over" another person or group. This is what we mean by power "over."

But how this "power over" works is complex. During medieval European feudalism, brute military force would impose the will of a feudal lord over his subjects. If a serf did not pay the portion of grain he owed to his lord who owned the land, a knight, armed with a sword, would show up at his door to take it from him. It was coercive power "over" in the most blatant sense. But the passage from feudalism to industrialization to the growth of urban centers, the birth of nation-states, and the organization of institutions of all kinds changed the way that power "over" is exercised. As Nietzsche would later describe "the will to power," it was exerted in multifarious ways and places all in the guise of morality and knowledge.[4]

Power Within

And so, after feudalism, power emerged differently. As cultural theorist Michel Foucault describes, power no longer relied on pure violence or military force to achieve its outcomes. Such overt violence was now broadly unacceptable in modern life. So power went "underground," from being exercised by one person (either personally or through an organization) *over* another via brute force, to being woven *within* a field of relations, a set of rules and practices, whether it be work, education, politics, or church. Each social system has its way of getting you to do things without overt violence.

Compliance is achieved by the powerful through discourses: ways of justifying the way things are. For example, institutions use science or ethics to justify that "this is just the way things are." When people need God, we go to church and learn to willingly submit to confession. When we have stress, we willingly go to a psychiatrist and submit to a body of knowledge that diagnoses us. When we get sick, we willingly go to the hospital and submit to the medical doctor under the guide of medical knowledge. We do what they tell us and we see ourselves as the patient. When we need money, we willingly apply for a job, work for an employer, and do what is expected of us by the boss and the banking systems. We vote in a democratic society, and afterward we will submit to the government and all that its leaders and laws tell us to do, including paying our taxes. The power exerted over us is accepted as legitimate, and we willingly cooperate with, if not defend, those in authority who tell us what to do. Over time, within these various practices, power becomes woven into how we conceive the way things work.[5] It is the way things are. All around us, we are continually being inducted into regimes of knowledge (religion, psychiatry, medicine, capitalism, etc.) in which we comply willingly with power.[6]

My very identity gets intertwined with these practices of power.[7] Being a cancer patient or a student or a professor or a Republican or a congressperson or an American citizen or a member of my church or a pastor becomes part of my identity. With that identity comes the power I must submit to or wield as part of who I am now. We become absorbed into discourses of power. The various practices we participate in condition us to believe that the power at work is just the way things are. And because we went to the hospital to get treatment for an ailment, or to the church to attain eternal life, we believe our complicity in these systems is our own idea.

If we are aware, we can see power at work in the many different discourses of life, from the local PTA to mental health awareness seminars to Facebook ads, Twitter clicks, the Internal Revenue Service, drug commercials, Medicare supplement plans, community policing, and on and on.[8] Each discourse or practice slots me into a role, creates expectations, shapes me to desire things, want a certain paycheck, want to be a certain kind of person and buy a certain product. It is all power being exerted by people "over" other people. And I am, for the most part, totally fine with it.

Ideology is used to justify economic power.[9] Various racist discourses justify exploiting Black persons, immigrants, indigenous peoples, and prison populations, suggesting these people are lazy, less intellectually gifted, less disciplined, incapable of studying hard, and immoral. This explains their (or our) plight. This explains why White persons climb to the top and enjoy so much of the economic wealth of our country. But it is all power being exerted by people "over" people, by institutions "over" persons, lodged "within" discourses and systems. And I am, if part of the advantaged group, totally fine with it.

Or am I? In recent decades we have become more aware of the power at work within the medical gaze (how medicine sees me), the male gaze (how my gender is shaped by how I'm seen), the racial gaze (how I am seen based on the color of my skin).[10] The phrases "mass incarceration" and "critical race theory" have gone mainstream, and there is resistance now to the ways our legal discourse exploits people of a certain color. #OccupyWallStreet, #BlackLivesMatter, #MeToo, and #ChurchToo are just some of the hashtags that remind us there are movements of people everywhere awakening to the abuses of power at work "within" the systems we inhabit. When a police officer shoots a Black person in the neighborhood, when a woman endures a sexual advance by her male boss, we no longer brush aside these acts and say, "It's just the way things are." We now work to expose and resist the abusive power "over" that is being revealed at work "within" the discourses. We are aware like never before of the layers of power "over" hidden "within" the systems we live in every day.

Power To

Feminists in North America after World War II provided a different view of power. Following in the steps of earlier feminist movements of the nineteenth and early twentieth centuries, which focused on the rights of women in relation to men, including the right to vote, access to education, and so on,[11] these feminists described power as the ability to achieve something, make an impact. This was power defined as empowerment, the "power to" do something.

Instead of power being articulated in "male" terms, as positional power "over" some persons in a field where actors are competing with one another for that power, these feminists preferred to define power as a generative force to accomplish goals within a relational network.[12] Today, many feminists of color, including womanist leaders, see power as the capacity/power to liberate oneself and one's people from cultural oppression so as to live an empowered life. They see power as empowerment.[13]

With this notion of "power to," feminists emphasized the equitable distribution of power as the means to accomplish justice. Let us distribute power as a resource more equitably among men and women, wives and husbands, persons of color and White persons, Black women and White women, and so forth.[14] Let us use power to empower others, making way for the empowerment of the marginalized. Let us distribute the "power to" control our lives, liberate persons, and participate in society unfettered by gender-based (and other) restrictions.

But is such a distribution of power even possible? Some third-wave feminists, hearkening to Foucault, argue that power doesn't work that way. Iris Marion Young, for example, argued that "bringing power under the logic of distribution" misconstrues what power is. It conceives of power "as a kind of stuff possessed by individual agents in greater or lesser amounts." But power is "a relation rather than a thing." Ultimately, she argues, power works within systems, practices, networks, and discourses, and those processes cannot be changed through distribution.[15]

Certainly there is "stuff" like money, corporate positions, and military resources that, if you have them, you can distribute them, and thereby you can affect the workings of power. But this "stuff" will remain controlled and managed within systems and ways of thinking. Moving around the stuff accomplishes very little if the systems and discourses in which they operate remain the same.

And then, of utmost importance, we must not forget there is still someone or some group who is actually doing the distributing of those power resources. And so the questions cannot be ignored: Who gets to decide the just distribution of power? What considerations should drive that decision? How do we ensure this exercise of power "over" is not another unjust act of coercion? Most importantly, does not moving around resources of power within the same system just perpetuate the same system's abusive power in another form?

Feminists like Young get pushback from other feminists who worry that her construal of power strips women of the agency and ability to effect justice.[16] But it is hard to deny the way power works within systems. There is no real empowerment for women without resistance to the power "over" at work within patriarchal systems. Any empowerment of one person entails that another person be the subject of that power. Indeed, the one who is liberated from the system of patriarchy, misogyny, or heteronormativity, from the "power over" at work that produces the oppression and domination, must exercise power over those systems and over persons of power in those systems. In the end, therefore, "power to" cannot help but become another form of "power over."

We see this often when a woman is given a position of power within a patriarchal system of men. Through no fault of her own, the domination that comes through the concentration of power in the hands of a few men at the top is not remedied by merely redistributing that same power to a woman. The system itself will find another way to perpetuate the same power relation and absorb women into it. The woman will take on the very character of male power over and become an abuser herself.[17] Merely redistributing power within the systems will not get at the injustices in the systems.[18]

Returning then to that church in Chicago, if I am empowered to have a voice, or a role, in that church, it will be within the power dynamics already ingrained in the culture of that church. I will in essence be a participant in those same power dynamics inherent to the church, its leadership, and the way things are done in that church. If indeed that power is abusive power over people, I will become complicit in it by being empowered in it. Which all is to say, we must recognize that "power to" do something, "within" a system, is still "power over" and requires all of us to discern it, how it works, and resist "power over" again and again.

Violence as the Revealing of Power Gone Bad

"Violence," typically, is defined as physical force that results in injury, abuse, trauma, or damage to one's person, property, and life. It is always negative, if not horrific. When a person pushes their power too far, and gets pushback in return, and then ego and narcissism take over, the person erupts with violence against the persons or groups that are resisting the power. Violence always reveals that "power over" has overstepped, going beyond its legitimacy.

Discerning violence, however, is not as easy as observing one person exerting a physical blow upon another person or seeing an army invading another country illegally and bombing its cities. There are different kinds of violence that abuse people and that don't entail visible physical violence at all.[19] If we have learned anything over the last several years in the thousands of abuse cases reported in churches, it is that abuse happens via power "within" systems. A predator grooms victims, thus setting them up for a false compliance with sexual violence. An abuser gaslights an abused person, making them believe it was their fault. Emotional abuse, verbal abuse, sexual abuse, racial or economic abuse can all happen without any direct evidence of physical violence. And yet there is still abuse and trauma. It was all still violence, perhaps a worse form of violence than if the person(s) had been physically injured.

Violence can be exercised in one's self-defense against violence. Victims of violence, in protecting themselves, will often perpetrate the same violence in retribution. The violence may be justified. And yet when the victim retaliates, that violence, in a sense, participates in the same evil being perpetrated upon the victim. Most often the violence will become magnified. And so this violence in self-defense can also be a "tell" of power gone bad. If we are to ever discern power, how it works, and when it goes wrong, we must understand how violence is part of the exercise of "power over" gone bad.

Cultural theorist Slavoj Žižek distinguishes between *subjective* violence and *objective* violence. He says subjective violence happens when a person inflicts a violent act against another person's or group of persons' physical well-being. A burglary, a terrorist act, and an act of domestic violence against one's spouse are examples of subjective violence. Objective violence, on the other hand, has no clear perpetrator. This is the violence woven into the system, the way the system works to enable (or even encourage) one person (or group) to exploit another. The economic laws that sustain a corrupt banking system; the system of public education, its well-defended curriculum, and the taxes to pay for it; stop-and-frisk laws that govern who is stopped by police and how, can all be examples of objective violence written into the system in which one lives.

Critical race theory explores how racism is written into the legal system. Rules, justifications, customs, courts, and appeals are all built in and justified in the system and exploit one group of people over another. It may go unseen by one group of people because that group benefits. This racism is justified within the system, but it is still violence. An act of subjective violence—a police shooting of a Black man or gang violence breaking out in a school—may get all the attention, while the objective violence, the system that breeds such overt acts, is ignored.[20]

Outbursts of physical violence (subjective violence), then, are often nothing less than the symptom of the systemic violence (objective violence) operating below the surface.[21] The continued revealing of senior pastors sexually abusing parishioners will never be dealt with just by dealing with the abusive pastor, or even by putting in guardrails and practices to keep the pastor in line. The "power over" woven within the system is being revealed and must be reshaped entirely. Whether it is "power over," "power within," or even "power to," violence and abuse are always a sign that these various forms of "power over" need to be challenged.

Power With

All this leads to a fourth kind of power, a power starkly different from the previous three, a power that I will label "power with." This is a power that refuses to exercise "power over" persons. Instead, this is a power of relationship, a power released in being "with" people. Whether you agree with a person or a group, whether they are your adversaries or not, is irrelevant. This is a power released in the mutuality between people. As a result, power "with" not only sees violence as a sign of power "over" going bad but views nonviolence as a posture through which true power "with" can actually work. And yet this power still gets things done. It just gets things done differently.

From Martin Luther King Jr. to Menno Simmons, Leo Tolstoy to Mahatma Gandhi, many theologians, artists, leaders, and justice activists have recognized the existence of this kind of power. Martin Luther King Jr. called it the "power of nonviolence." This power is released as we engage injustice through relationship, person-to-person presence, people-to-people encounter. We enter conflicts never to humiliate an opponent but to win a friendship. There is a true force at work in the space between persons that overcomes hate. King called it "love." For King, there is power in this dynamic. We who are nonviolent resisters of injustice, who enter these spaces with love, refusing to participate in the evil systems, throw a wrench into the machinery of injustice and, by so doing, make space for something new to begin. There is a sense that God is at work in this world for justice and that we can participate in it via "power with."[22]

These themes in King's power of nonviolence appear regularly among contemporary theorists. Queer theorist Judith Butler argues there is a force in nonviolence. For her, relationality, interdependency, and vulnerability are the conditions for the thriving of human life.[23] So being present with your body in vulnerability in the face of conflict can expose the ways we are mutually interrelated and then make space for working together for human thriving.[24] A power is released in this nonviolent with-ness that works for goodness and life.

Cornel West contrasts "weak" and "feeble" forms of power with the monarchical, corporate, patriarchal, or homophobic forms of power. Spiritual, moral power emanates from "women's power, or black power, or workers' power . . . people from below."[25] This is "power with," and, for West, there is a stark difference between this power "with" and power "over" that comes "from above being imposed on those below."

Multitudes of authors testify on the merits of "power with."

Mahatma Gandhi preached that nonviolent, embodied relational presence—what he called the practice of *Satyagraha*—releases a convicting power. He said this power, based in love, not fear, is "a thousand times more effective" than coercive power, what I'm naming "power over."[26]

Gustavo Gutiérrez, the Latin American liberation theologian, showed that God prefers to work among the powerless, who do not have access to "power over." Because of their openness and desperation for God's power, they are able to know and cooperate with God's power, "power with."[27] Gutiérrez calls this God's "preferential option for the poor," an "epistemological privilege" among the poor.[28]

Queer novelist Sarah Schulman, in her important book *Conflict Is Not Abuse*, describes how the diagnosis and use of the term "abuse" can itself set one person "over" the other, short-circuiting the working out of conflict and setting the relationship into ongoing patterns of abusive "power over." Mutuality, or being with each other, is the defining element for whether the relationship is in a conflict or entwined in an act of abusive power.[29] For Schulman, discerning the difference between "power with" and "power over" (my words) is essential to repairing interpersonal and social relationships.

All of these thinkers bear testimony to the existence of a different kind of power at work in the world that is an alternative to "power over." This "power with" is released via personal embodied presence, relationality, love, mutuality. This power refuses to coerce or participate in the coercion of "power over."

The Inherent Temptation to Default to "Power Over"

"Power over" is prone to abuse and violence. The abuse and violence are, every time, a sign that we are on the wrong side of power. "Power within" and "power to" are legitimated forms of "power over," and so these ways of power are also prone to being the wrong side of power. "Power with," however, stands in contrast to these other forms of power, and so we are tempted to believe that the problems of "power over" are solved by choosing to exercise power via "power with."

And yet history shows that "power with" often degenerates regularly into "power over."

For instance, the liberation theology movements of Latin America in the '60s and '70s began by being "with" the oppressed. The base ecclesial communities of the Roman Catholic Church worked through real presence via communities of resistance to withstand the dictatorship regimes of late twentieth-century Latin America.[30] And yet eventually these movements found themselves justifying violence to accomplish economic goals.[31] Cardinal Ratzinger, along with Pope John Paul II, had to warn these movements of the violence inherent to the Marxist logic they had adopted.[32] At the Extraordinary Synod of Bishops in Rome in November 1985, conservative Colombian bishop Darío Castrillón Hoyos aimed criticism at them, saying, "When I see a church with a machine gun, I cannot see the crucified Christ in that church."[33] Putting aside the righteousness of their causes, even these movements, which began with profound presence with the poor, devolved into violence and "power over" in their later histories.[34]

The civil rights movements of the 1950s and 1960s began as a movement of nonviolence. As we have seen, Martin Luther King Jr. founded the movement on the "power of nonviolence." A few years in, however, Stokely Carmichael and James Forman argued with King over the tactics of nonviolence. They grew impatient with nonviolent love. Carmichael saw nonviolence as a tactic to be employed only if it was being effective. He eventually argued for discarding it in favor of Black Power, "fighting back," and the taking of justice "into our own hands."[35] The nonviolent leadership of John Lewis came under attack in the Student Nonviolent Coordinating Committee (SNCC), a founding organization of the early years of the civil rights movement. Lewis was ousted as chairman of SNCC, and their emphasis on nonviolent relational community organizing began to decline.[36] The movement over time moved its work entirely to the work of national legislation.[37] "Power with" was replaced with forms of "power over."

American business leadership saw the value of "power with" as the means to leading corporations in the 1980s and 1990s. Servant leadership became popular among CEOs. Its guru, Robert Greenleaf, preached that serving "with" the people you lead in mutuality produces flourishing for all parts of your business. He argued for practices of listening, empathy, healing relationships, and dialogue as ways of leadership versus positional decision-making.[38] But as this approach became more mainstream, it became a tactic for increasing productivity and making more money.[39] It became a "technique" to manipulate and manage people toward better profitability.[40] It migrated to becoming another form of "power over."

The question, then, is whether "power with" can only ever be yet another tactic (Stokely Carmichael) to gain power "over" a person or a group of persons.[41] And if indeed "power over" is always prone to violence and inflicting abuse and trauma, is there any managing of it? Escaping it? Is a right side of power even possible?

As we turn to the next chapter, we will see that "power with" can be an alternative to "power over" only if it operates on completely different terms than "power over." It must be another kind of power entirely. We will see that ultimately there is no right side of "power over" for the Christian who follows Jesus. Therefore, for the Christian to be on the wrong side of "power over," refusing it altogether, is to be on the right side. Instead, the side of godly power, released in the person and work of Jesus, by the Holy Spirit, is the right side.

For Jesus Himself has unleashed an entirely different power at work in the world, and we who follow Jesus submit to His power alone.[42]

Imagine with Me

Returning to that encounter in the Sunday morning church service in Chicago, imagine if that church could operate via "power with" as opposed to "power over." What would your first encounter with that church be like?

I imagine my first encounter with that church would not be in that Sunday morning service. Instead, perhaps I met Christians from the church for the first time at the local clothes exchange through either exchanging clothes or working at the exchange itself. Or perhaps I worked alongside someone from the church at the local school to overcome problems children are having with learning or getting a good meal. Maybe we just met at the local game room in town. And now we're in a McDonald's, a coffee shop, or at a neighborhood backyard. A person sitting at a table across from me, perhaps sipping a cup of coffee, would be listening to me, asking questions about me in a noncoercive way. I'm experiencing a strange, warm presence, not an agenda. I'm sensing a movement of the Spirit, but I don't know why, nor even that this is the Spirit of God at work.

The most important weekly meeting of this church probably would take place sitting around a table of people, in a home, or gathering with a group of men in a bowling alley, and I would have been invited to share a meal, share life struggles, and pray. Certainly, the church would have a Sunday gathering, but my first encounter with that church wouldn't be at that gathering. Because the true power of the with-ness of Jesus requires that the power of His presence be most easily encountered first at a table in the neighborhood.

When I finally do go to a Sunday morning gathering, I would already know several people and would sit with them. The preaching pastor for that Sunday would stand amid the gathering to preach, assuming a posture not "over" the congregation but among the congregation. The Word would be preached with power, but it would not be an authoritarian power "over," but a power of conviction of the Spirit already at work among a people. From top to bottom, the experience of power would be different from that first encounter of church I talked about at the outset of this chapter.

Is such a "power with" even possible—a power that does not devolve into "power over"? What defines this "power with"? What makes it possible? To this question we now turn.

2

Worldly Power and God's Power

There Are Two Powers, Not One

> You know that among the Gentiles . . . their rulers lord it over them. . . . But it is not so among you.
>
> Mark 10:42–43

I once met with a man who cared deeply for single people who struggled with loneliness, past relationship abuses, and an inability to connect in dating settings. I'll call him George. He had some innovative and daring ideas that he wanted to put to the test in starting a ministry for these persons. Over a cup of coffee, he shared with me his hopes to start this ministry and asked if I thought this ministry would be accepted in our church. I responded by saying, "I don't know why not." For sure I had some questions, how he'd go about it, but I was sure he would be welcome in our church.

As one of the pastors of our church, I sought to encourage ministries to spring up out of the work of the Spirit as discerned by gifted leaders. And so I encouraged him to cultivate this ministry from the ground up, use his gifts, pray much, and seek the Spirit. I suggested that he meet with people over cups of coffee in the same way he and I were meeting. Church leadership would support him, pray with him, give him feedback, give help as needs arose. But George must be the one to lead, allowing the Holy Spirit to work and bring forth fruit. If signs of the Spirit were evident, and the ministry grew, the church would recognize that and facilitate more. But this ministry of his must be the work of God among us, not merely his own pet project.

As things evolved, however, George wanted the pastors and elders to get behind his ministry before it had barely begun. He asked us to endorse the ministry, put church resources behind it, enlist people to join it, and advertise it via communications while many of the pastors and elders were not even comfortable with what George was proposing yet. There was even an accusation in the congregation against George's leadership that George needed to resolve. And so, even though it was our practice to encourage new ministries, making space for the Spirit to work among us, it would be the fruit of the ministry that would be the source of its affirmation. And George would need to listen and resolve the conflict he had with a member of the congregation. The pastors and elders were not comfortable providing George what he was asking for. George took this as the pastors withholding their support of him.

I can remember George addressing me directly in a leadership meeting. He told me, "You have power and you should use it to back my ministry." I responded by saying I had a few concerns about George's ministry. But even if I had no concerns, I reject using power that way. I believe we allow and submit to the work of God's power among us, listen, discern, participate, and lead. And as God's power causes a gift and a ministry to flourish, we (and I emphasize it's a "we") recognize and support it as best we can. If there are accusations, God will use those too to either discipline the ministry or grow it even more.

George said I wasn't recognizing the power I already carried just by walking in the room. I said that power dynamic may be true, but I believe that power dynamic is of the world. As a follower of Jesus, I give up that power, refusing to wield it. I choose intentionally to submit to God's power. Any perceived power "over" I disavow and instead submit all I'm doing to the power of God at work among us as we work together.

"Under Power"

George's thinking on power is common today. Most people in the West operate as if power is power and leadership is about who has it and who will use it for the right purposes. It is what I have called the standard account of power. I, on the other hand, was wary of "power over." Over the years I had seen its damage to persons and leaders alike, no matter how well-meaning the persons were who were employing it. Instead, I was seeing that there are two distinct kinds of power: worldly "power over" and godly "power with." As a leader in the church, I was seeking to reject "power over" in my ministry and our church. I was suspicious of anyone claiming to be on the right side of it. I was pursuing imperfectly to live "under" God's power, the power of the living Christ at work among us by the Spirit.

For me, then, there ultimately is no "power with" that is not "under power" of another kind. Living "under" God's power, in submission to God's power, actually enables a leader to lead "with" the power of God, as manifested among a people. Living "under" God's power rejects worldly power. I do not seek to exercise "power over" people as if I know what is best. Instead, submitting to God's power among a people, via the posture of being "under" His reign, I am able to enter a space of God's power working among us, and then cooperate.

For me, in that moment with George, "power over" would never be overcome unless there was a fundamental change to the relationship of all of us to that power. I, as human agent, must give up control of worldly power and submit myself to being "under" God's power so that we could discern and become people used by God together. "Under power" makes possible "power with" in a way that displaces all other human "power over."

There is real danger here in stating the issue of power in this way. A White male, not acknowledging his worldly power, can allow himself to act and behave in a way that does not take responsibility for the worldly power inherent in his actions and words. He can abuse persons without intending to. It is much better, many would say, for the person in power, and for those under that person's power, to simply acknowledge the power, get that out in the open, and discern the proper use of that power prayerfully, and then distribute that power for righteous purposes.

But there is an alternative option. Instead of employing worldly power, I could recognize that God is calling me, as a leader, to come under His power, and cooperate with His work among a people. Instead of taking the reins of worldly power, I could reject that power entirely and instead take the posture of "under" God's power. By so doing, I would make space for godly power to work in ways that by His Spirit relationally connect, reconcile, convince, heal, and guide people and their lives together. This opens up a whole other side of power, what I'd call the right side of power.

When we adopt this perspective, God works among us in ways we could not have thought of and with outcomes that are transforming. "Under power" releases among us a different kind of power altogether, a power that is "able to accomplish abundantly far more than all we can ask or imagine" (Eph. 3:20).[1]

It is true that worldly "power over" can still be employed for good purposes, if limited purposes, with the right management and accountability. But it is fraught with danger and it limits what God can do. I viewed myself, a pastor, taking up "power over," as putting myself in charge of worldly power in the name of God. To do this is to endanger not only myself but everyone in my path. Instead, I believe the church leader should lay down worldly power entirely, refusing to exercise it, and instead lead a people into a coming "under" God's power, a mutuality of submission to God, and a participation with Him in God's power at work among us.

Once I realized there was a distinct difference between worldly "power over" and God's power among, the issue between George and me was stark. I had to take account of my own self in relation to the coercive effects of power. I believed there were two powers at work in the world, and I had to choose between them. George believed there was one. And to me this made all the difference.

There Are Two Powers, Not One

We have seen in the previous chapter the many versions of power and how they are all in essence versions of "power over." Even "power with," as valiant as it may be at enlisting people's joint participation in power, is prone to being manipulated by a leader or group for an agenda. It too can become "power over," leaving abuse in its wake. "Power with" can be an alternative to "power over" only if it operates on completely different terms than "power over." "Power with," which cannot be manipulated by human persons to exert "power over," must put humans in submission to an alternative power that is not theirs to control: the transcendent power of God. Only by surrendering first to God's power in Christ by the Spirit, thereby coming "under" God's power, can I then participate in a power that is truly "power with."[2]

As a result, instead of using "power over," a leader must give up power and come "under" another power, the power of God (Phil. 2:4–8). It is in the leader's submission to the power of God that godly power can be released by God among a people and then followed. These are the dynamics at work that I shall describe as "under power." "Under power" makes space for another kind of power, altogether different from "worldly power." It is in essence the terms by which there can be an alternative to worldly power.

To come "under power" requires that we see another form of power at work that is altogether different from worldly power. There is (1) worldly power, which works "over" people via a position, a discourse of justification, or other kind of coercion, and (2) godly power, at work through the presence and power of Jesus by the Spirit among a group of people.

Godly power demands a complete upending of power "over." Its release is located in persons willingly coming under the reign and authority of the living God. It births God's work among and with a people. As Stanley Hauerwas reminds us, "God does not rule creation through coercion, but through a cross."[3] This is the way God chooses (as we will soon see) to work in His power. The power that is released by God cannot be manipulated by human persons to exert "power over." Any such attempt will fail because once any person or group claims to exercise "power over" in the name of God, the power is no longer God's, because God's power, by definition, cannot be controlled, only cooperated with.

Exercising worldly "power over" in the name of God is the ultimate dangerous form of power. Certainly "power over" is always fraught with the potential for abuse. But when we blur worldly power with godly power, proclaiming that what we do "over" people we do for God in God's name and for His purposes, we unhinge it from any restraints under the illusion that God is doing it. This defines ultimately the wrong side of power.

"Worldly power" with no restraints, acting in the name and authority of God, is the recipe for abuse of the worst kinds. It is the great temptation of Satan rejected by Christ Himself in the desert: seeking to accomplish God's purposes via worldly power (Matt. 4:8–10). It is the first sin of the garden: seeking to usurp God (Gen. 3:22).

Ultimately, then, true "power with" must be a power that causes humans to give up "power over" in order to be under God's power and thus be enabled to participate in "power with" God. "Power with" can be different from "power over" only via "under power."[4] This relation between "power with" and "under power" explains just how different worldly power and godly power are. It defines for the Christian what it means to be on the right side of power.

The Scriptures Bear Witness to the Two Powers

The Scriptures bear witness to the two powers. They tell a continual story of God inviting His people to submit to His power and join with Him in His power as He works for the healing of the world.

Jesus

Beginning with Jesus's words "not so among you" (Mark 10:43), it could not be any more in-your-face. After Jesus tells His disciples how He must suffer, James and John, in a most glaring moment of misunderstanding, start to jockey for position in the coming kingdom (v. 37). They want a part in the worldly "power over" that they assume will surely be theirs once Jesus assumes the mantle of the reign of David in Jerusalem. But Jesus bluntly informs them that they do not know what they're asking (v. 38). As the other disciples get agitated at James and John's power grab, Jesus tells them in no uncertain terms, "You know that among the Gentiles those whom they recognize as their rulers lord it *over* them, and their great ones are tyrants *over* them. But it is not so among you; but whoever wishes to become great among you must be your servant, and whoever wishes to be first among you must be slave of all" (vv. 42–44). Jesus acknowledges two powers.[5] One power is of the world, "over" people; the other is of His kingdom and is released in serving from the posture of "under."

In Luke 22, as Jesus celebrates the Passover supper with His disciples, contemplating the suffering that is to come in Jerusalem, a dispute similar to the one in the Mark 10 episode breaks out. Jesus instructs His disciples again with similar words around the table, saying this "power over" shall "not [be] so with you" (Luke 22:24–27). He includes being a "benefactor" as a mode of power that shall also be excluded from the kingdom (v. 25). And so, all modes of "power over," including those that use charity to exert patronage, shall be excluded from our new life together. Instead, Jesus says, "I confer on you . . . a kingdom," a kingdom of a different sort (v. 29).

If we take John 13 to be an account of this same Passover meal (an interpretation that is somewhat in dispute), it is significant that Jesus washed His disciples' feet that evening, displaying the way of this kingdom's rule, where power is released through submissional service, mutuality, and the posture of "under." Though Jesus is "Lord and Teacher," He sets "an example" (vv. 14–15). Unless the disciples do this, they can have "no share with" Jesus in His power and transforming work (v. 8). There could not be a starker contrast of the power released in Jesus versus the power He denounces as of the world.

Throughout His life Jesus resists the evil powers that dominate over persons. He cast out demons that destroy lives. His miracles of healing and His exorcisms display a different kind of power, one not available to political authorities.[6] He refuses the crowds that rally around Him, ready for a political insurrection. He teaches via presence, not platforms. He confronts Pharisees with disarming words. He sides with the poor and the powerless. He pronounces blessings on the poor in spirit, those who mourn, the meek, those who hunger and thirst. Here the kingdom shall be made manifest, He says. Each time, He either illustrates or exercises power through His presence, by the Spirit of God, through words that connect, through the power of deep conviction, illumination, never "power over."

When faced with the ultimate manifestations of "power over," Jesus rejects them in stark ways. In the desert He rejects Satan's offers of worldly empires, "their glory and all this authority" (Luke 4:6). When Peter draws his sword (Luke 22:49–51; cf. John 18:10) and cuts off the ear of a servant of the high priest, Jesus rebukes him and heals the ear. When Jesus stands before the full brunt of worldly power, the Roman governor Pontius Pilate, questioning Jesus as to whether He claims to be king of the Jews, Jesus replies, "My kingdom is not from this world. If my kingdom were from this world, my followers would be fighting to keep me from being handed over to the Jews. But as it is, my kingdom is not from here" (John 18:36). Jesus is contrasting the worldly power of Pilate with the power of His kingdom, the "power over" of Pilate to the "under power" posture that releases "power with" God.

This power is demonstrated in the disciples' missionary journey in Luke 10. Upon returning, they report to Jesus, "Lord, in your name even the demons submit to us!" (v. 17). People are being healed, delivered from evil powers, restored to life. Jesus responds in ecstasy, saying with joy, "I watched Satan fall from heaven like a flash of lightning. See, I have given you authority to tread on snakes and scorpions, and over all the power of the enemy; and nothing will hurt you" (vv. 18–19). This is real godly transformative power. But Jesus cautions them, "Nevertheless, do not rejoice at this, that the spirits submit to you, but rejoice that your names are written in heaven" (v. 20). The disciples are always having to be reminded that this is not something they did via a worldly power under their control. Rather, as subjects of the King, they have their names written in heaven, and they are "under his power" and have been made participants in the kingdom's power of God.

Jesus is always having to teach the disciples about a different kind of power that does not work as worldly power under their control. When He comes down from the transfiguration, He is confronted by a crowd arguing and the reality of a convulsing boy whom the disciples could not heal. Jesus decries their lack of trust (Mark 9:19) and heals the boy. The disciples are flustered, asking, "Why could we not cast it out?" (v. 28). They want to know why they could not control the power. Jesus replies simply, "This kind can come out only through prayer" (v. 29). This kind of evil cannot be overcome with human worldly power, but only through the power of God. And you therefore must make space for God to work through prayer, dependence, and trust, through coming "under" the power of God so as to participate in His work.

On the first day after the resurrection, according to John 20, Jesus appears to the disciples and sends them out into the world as His representatives (v. 21). He breathes on them, and they receive the Holy Spirit. Then He says, "If you forgive the sins of any, they are forgiven them; if you retain the sins of any, they are retained" (v. 23). They are given the keys of the kingdom to break people free from the chains of sin and death (Matt. 16:14–19). This kingdom's power is in the forgiveness of sins, the dislodging of the powers. It is released via the work of the Holy Spirit. It is God's power, not of this world.

Before Pilate, Jesus is distinguishing between the power of armies, physical coercion, and force over people, on the one hand, and the way godly power works with and among a people and social systems in His kingdom, on the other. And so it would be a mistake to consider this godly power of Jesus as purely a personal spiritual power working upon the inner souls of people. This is a power of a kingdom set loose among political social realities, transforming the way people live together.[7] In this way, Jesus sets the terms for understanding power for Christians. The choice to use worldly power is either sin or the result of sin. For Jesus, it could not be clearer: there are two powers, not one. And His followers must choose to live under the power of God.

Genesis

We start with Jesus and the Gospels, and Jesus, the full revelation of God, must guide how we read the creation accounts. Yet we must also consider how power is viewed in the rest of Scripture, going all the way back to Genesis 1–3, where so many evangelicals and Protestants ground their theologies of power.

On the sixth day God creates humankind and says, "Let them have dominion over" the fish, birds, cattle, wild animals, and every creeping thing on the earth (Gen. 1:26). A few verses later, God commands male and female to "be fruitful and multiply, and fill the earth and subdue it; and have dominion over" the fish, birds, cattle, wild animals, and every living thing (v. 28). God seems to invite humans to exert a "power over" in His creation. The God of Genesis seems to contradict Jesus on the use of "power over."

But Old Testament scholar Theodore Hiebert reminds us that God created humans in His image (Gen. 1:26). Humans are to exercise power, but in the same way that God does. God's image is described as plural: "in our image, according to our likeness." God is relational. And, according to Hiebert, already in the original Hebrew there is a sense of the way God rules within an interdependent order through His presence among. Any notion of "power over" in this Genesis account, therefore, must be placed within the broader context of a world created within the interdependence of relations as inhabited by God's presence.[8]

This is substantiated by the second account of God creating humanity, in Genesis 2. Here humanity is formed from the dust of the earth (2:7) and given the command to farm it (v. 15). Hiebert translates the key word describing what humans are to do as "farm it" or "cultivate it" and argues that this has the sense of "serving" the earth. In contrast to ruling "over" creation in human terms, humans are created from the earth and are interdependent within it, to serve it, and live in the presence and fullness of the power of God.

It is not until the fall, in Genesis 3, that we see a distinctively alternative kind of power emerge. Here Adam and Eve, living in dependence upon the presence of God, are tempted to "be like God" (3:5). They disobey God, eating of the fruit of the tree of knowledge of good and evil, and separate themselves relationally from God. They now hide from "the presence of the LORD God among the trees of the garden" (v. 8). They are distanced from each other as well and are now ashamed of their nakedness. Relational interdependence is broken. A new, blatant "power over" appears. The husband "shall rule over" the woman (v. 16). The man must now toil over the earth to eat the fruits of it. In their act of rebellion, humans have sought to be God, usurp God (v. 22). They are expelled from the garden to live with this new fallen "power over," and the earth is soon to be "filled with violence" (6:11).

There are, of course, other accounts, grounded in evolutionary biology/anthropology, that narrate how humans evolved from egalitarian cultures to hierarchical, class-based societies. They suggest that evolutionary selection and group-based dynamics evolved human life into hierarchy.[9] The book of Genesis, however, as well as the rest of the biblical story, describes the origins of "power over" as based in sin.

And so the Genesis accounts of creation contrast two distinct kinds of power: the power of God at work among humanity in the garden and the "power over" of sin, which humanity exercises in rebellion against God, usurping His power and seeking autonomy. Humanity was created to thrive in God's presence. The garden was the sanctuary of God's presence.[10] Before the fall, there was only godly power, and humans were created to live under God's power and with God's power. Then came rebellion against God and the pursuit of autonomy, and a whole different power, a coercive "power over," enters the world.

There are two powers now, not one. And the way to God's fullest purposes for humanity is to reject the temptation of the garden and come "under" God's power at work among us all over again. This is what has been made possible in the person and work of Jesus Christ.

The Monarchy of Israel

Israel's long journey from Egypt to the promised land charts the people's submission to the living presence of God among them. As they journeyed through the wilderness, they were led by God's presence, manifest in the mobile tabernacle carried along with them. And yet Israel committed horrific

53

violence in the conquest. And so two distinct powers are at work in the history of Israel.

Nowhere is the difference between the two powers starker than in the rise of Israel's monarchy. Israel wanted to have a king like the surrounding nations had. It was Israel succumbing to the temptation of worldly power. In Deuteronomy 17:14–20, God actually gives permission to Israel to have a king, but He puts numerous restrictions upon this king.[11] This king shall not exalt himself above other members of the community. He must not acquire many horses, wives, and silver and gold as the other nations do. He must rule, in essence, to uphold God's rule in Israel. If God is to allow a king, it would *not* be a king who rules like a gentile king, but a king who rules as God rules via "power with."

In Judges 8–9, Gideon wins a battle over the Midianite kings. The Israelites, in grandiose hubris, attempt to make Gideon a king over them. They say, "Rule over us, you and your son and your grandson also; for you have delivered us out of the hand of Midian" (8:22). Gideon rejects this suggestion, saying, "I will not rule over you, and my son will not rule over you; the Lord will rule over you" (v. 23). Gideon rejects "power over" for God's rule and His way of ruling among a people.

In 1 Samuel 8, God grants Israel a king. Before this, it appears that God preferred to rule Israel without a king (despite Deut. 17). Israel was governed with a group of leaders in mutuality, including judges, elders, priests, and prophets all in relation to each other. There was no singular, centralized leader. All the leaders functioned in a role and were accountable mutually and to God.[12] In 1 Samuel 8, however, the people of Israel ask Samuel for a king "like other nations" (8:5). Samuel is displeased. God describes this request as a rejection of His power. "Listen to the voice of the people," He tells Samuel, "for they have not rejected you, but they have rejected me from being king over them" (v. 7). So God grants them a king as a concession but warns them of what is coming. "These will be the ways of the king who will reign over you: he will take your sons and appoint them to his chariots . . . and he will appoint for himself commanders. . . . He will take your daughters to be perfumers and cooks and bakers. He will take the best of your fields" (vv. 11–18). He will enslave people and confiscate the people's fields. But despite all these warnings, the people "are determined to have a king over" them so that they "may be like other nations" (vv. 19–20).

So Israel, presented with the way of God's power versus the way of worldly "power over," chooses worldly power. They choose a king. It does not go well. Time after time, the chosen king, who starts out following God, becomes an idol unto himself, oppressing the people and leading Israel into wars. This was the way of the surrounding nations. The kings even import the ways of violence and war from the nations.[13] It is the lesson of the two powers. There are two powers, worldly power and godly power, and whenever the two powers are blurred, and God's people take up worldly power in God's name, abuse and destruction are not far behind. Jesus's words now become all the more pronounced when He describes worldly power in terms of the way the gentiles "lord it over them." But for Jesus, "it shall not be so among you" (Mark 10:43).

Violence in the Old Testament: The Ultimate Blurring of "Power Over" as Exercised by God?

No narration of the biblical history of power can ignore the horrific violence attributed to God in the Old Testament. The God of Israel, who is a "God merciful and gracious, slow to anger, and abounding in steadfast love and faithfulness, keeping steadfast love for the thousandth generation, forgiving iniquity and transgression and sin" (Exod. 34:6–7), appears to order His very own people to take on worldly power and commit unspeakable atrocities. The God who repudiates violence, works for peace (Mic. 4:3), "makes wars cease" by His presence (Ps. 46:9), who compels His people to put no trust in armies or weapons but to trust Him for protection (2 Kings 6; Hosea 10:13–14; Isa. 31:1), somehow commands Israel to devote to destruction by the edge of the sword "all in the city, both men and women, young and old" (Josh. 6:21), to destroy the Amalekites, killing men and women and children and all living things (1 Sam. 15:3), and commit genocidal acts and rape in His name (Num. 21:2; 31:17, 35; Deut. 2:24; 20:16; 21:10–14). How is this possible?

A full treatment of the violence in the Old Testament is not possible here. Suffice it to say that the work of scholars like Gregory Boyd, William Webb, and John Nugent illumines how to read the Old Testament in view of the two powers.[14] Boyd begins with the ways Jesus reveals how God works as He enters into the world, taking on the sin and violence of the world in order to redeem and restore the world. Boyd calls this cruciform accommodation. The Old Testament tells the story of the same God entering the world of sin and violence, often having acts of violence attributed to Him in the process. Boyd says God "was willing to stoop as far as necessary to remain in solidarity with his people" so as to work among them for their ultimate salvation.[15] This is who God is and the way God works. This is "power with" in all its vulnerability. At the same time, because God stoops to be with His people, acts of violence get mistakenly attributed to Him. Through the lens of the crucified God, however, we can see something deeper going on in each act of horrific violence attributed to God. The Israelites are blurring the two powers (a theme we'll get to in the next chapter). They are ascribing to God the ways of worldly "power over," not trusting in the power of God.

Boyd leads us through episodes where it appears God perpetrates horrific violence, but in reality God is being implicated in the projections of Israel and its leaders. For instance, after fighting numerous battles, Israel inhabits Canaan and then celebrates with a first meal. In the following section, Joshua looks up and sees a man standing in front of him with a drawn sword in his hand. Surprised and threatened, he asks, "Are you one of us, or one of our adversaries?" This man, who later identifies himself as "commander of the army of the LORD," replies, "Neither" (Josh. 5:13–14). Stunningly, before the battle of Jericho, after many violent battles have already been won, God (through His angel) reveals Himself as one who does not make enemies or take sides. Indeed, He is not the "violent god" ordering the genocides.[16] He is revealed as not the one Joshua assumes Him to be.

In Joshua 11, Joshua kills all the people of the kingdoms of Hazor, "as Moses the servant of the LORD had commanded" (Josh. 11:12).[17] Boyd, depending heavily on Walter Brueggemann, carefully shows how Joshua legitimizes each act of violence not by appealing to the word of God that he heard directly from God but by appealing four times to the older authority of Moses (vv. 12, 15, 20, 23). God Himself actually only authorizes the hamstringing of the horses and the burning of the chariots, which were the tools of war (v. 6). Boyd leads us through story after story of Old Testament violence, revealing clues or subtle contradictions in the text that suggest it was not God authorizing the horrific violence of worldly power but rather the leaders attributing the acts of worldly power to God.

And so, by reading the Old Testament with this understanding of God's ways of power, we can see how violence is attributed to God as an accommodation to ancient Near Eastern cultural assumptions about the way the nations' gods work. Instead of the Old Testament supporting the idea that

God works through the violence of worldly power, the violence in the Old Testament instructs us how godly power can be blurred with worldly power and how worldly power turns horrific when blurred with godly power and done in God's name—a subject we will turn to extensively in the next chapter.

The Servant Songs of Isaiah

During the time of Babylonian captivity, the servant songs of Isaiah 42, 49, 52, and 53 appear in the history of Israel. They depict a future leader for Israel who shall lead the nations. But this leader shall not be a king of worldly power like the gentiles have. Instead, this leader is to depend upon God alone (Isa. 49:4–5). This leader will be rejected by all humanity (Isa. 52–53). He is abused. He sacrifices himself in accepting the punishment due others. He "was wounded for our transgressions, crushed for our iniquities; upon him was the punishment that made us whole, and by his bruises we are healed" (53:5). So different from Cyrus, who ruled by coercion and dominion over his enemies, this suffering servant-king will lead as one among the people, via godly power, and victory shall come (v. 12).

The suffering servant of Isaiah is the archetype of a power arising out of Israel that is radically different from any power known by the nations. The songs of the suffering servant reconfigure what kingship shall mean in contrast to kingship among the gentiles. This king will not be a leader who will dominate the world through coercive military force. God surely can use Cyrus—or allow the force of Cyrus to be used for judgment as the consequences of one's sins. But even though Cyrus shall be used by God (Isa. 45:1–7), this does not excuse Assyria of its own sins. For God also allows Babylon to punish Assyria, Persia to punish Babylon.[18] And so God allows worldly "power over" to play out as judgment, but this "power over" cannot redeem or transform. Coercion and force work against true healing and transformation. Only the "power with" of God's power can work to heal and transform. And this will be made manifest to us as we come "under" His power.

The suffering servant, prophesied in Isaiah, is the full manifestation of this way of power and is fulfilled in the coming of Jesus. The songs of the suffering servant reveal there are two powers, not one, and God shall surely work through His power to redeem and save the world. In the words of the prophet Zechariah, "Not by might, nor by power, but by my spirit, says the LORD of hosts" (Zech. 4:6).

The Apostle Paul

Returning to the New Testament, we find that Paul, the apostolic founder and leader of the gentile churches, is the example par excellence of one who leads "under power." He surely could have been justified in leading from a posture of "over," but he refused. Rejecting the way of "lofty words or [worldly] wisdom," he came "in weakness . . . with a demonstration of the Spirit and of power, so that your faith might rest not on human wisdom but on the power of God." He "decided to know nothing among [them] except Jesus Christ, and him crucified" (1 Cor. 2:1–5). When he had difficult things to say to his churches, he preferred "love in a spirit of gentleness" versus the "stick" (4:21).

In 1 Corinthians 3, Paul chastises the Corinthians for operating via "power over," with "jealousy and quarreling" among them, and for "behaving according to human inclinations." He labels it living "of the flesh" (3:3). For Paul this is incomprehensible. Do they not know they are the temple of God, the dwelling place of the power of His presence? But they settle for the power of the world. It is all a stunning description of the two powers vying for the allegiance of the Corinthians.

Perhaps because he refuses to take a posture "over" his churches, Paul finds himself having to defend his apostleship. After all, he refuses to demand support from the churches (2 Cor. 11:7–9). He works with his hands, alongside other workers, always calling them colaborers, coworkers, brothers and sisters (1 Cor. 3:9; Phil. 2:25; 4:3; 1 Thess. 3:2; Philem. 24).[19] Though he is tempted to boast of his credentials, he prefers to "boast of the things that show [his] weakness" (2 Cor. 11:30). And so he does not live up to any of the markers of hierarchical privilege that all other Roman leaders wield.[20] As a result, people are calling Paul's apostleship into question.

In response, Paul refuses the posture of "power over." Instead, he bears a thorn as a mark of his apostleship, to keep him from being proud and heavy-handed. He chooses to live under the power of the Lord, who has said, "My grace is sufficient for you, for [my] power is made perfect in weakness." So, the apostle declares he will boast all the more of his weaknesses, so that "the power of Christ" may dwell in him (2 Cor. 12:9). All of this makes Paul an exemplar of the way godly power works via a posture of "under power."

When Paul turns to expounding the dynamics of godly power set loose in Christ, he recites the great Christ hymn found in Philippians 2:5–11. Although Christ "existed in the form of God," He "did not regard equality with God as something to be exploited" (v. 6). Christ gave up any position over and instead "emptied himself, taking the form of a slave, being born in human likeness" (v. 7). It was when Christ humbled Himself, going to the cross in obedience, that God released His power through Him and exalted Him to the name above all names.

According to New Testament scholar Michael Gorman, the first sentence of the Philippians hymn should be translated "because he was God . . ." rather than "though he was God. . . ."[21] In other words, Christ gave up worldly power in order to come among us, be with us in human vulnerable flesh, and be crucified and receive the violence and sin and death of the world upon Himself instead of inflicting those things upon humanity, because this is the very nature of God. This is the way God's power works. Godly power and the way His power works are defined in stark contrast to worldly power.

The choice between godly power and worldly power runs through Paul's Epistles. For Paul, godly power is a way of living, not merely a sociological reality. As he describes in Philippians 3:8–10, "For his sake I have suffered the loss of all things, and I regard them as rubbish, in order that I may gain Christ. . . . I want to know Christ and the power of his resurrection and the sharing of his sufferings by becoming like him in his death."

The Book of Revelation

For many Christians, the Revelation of John, the last book of Scripture, is a picture of God's power being exerted in the final judgment of His wrath. The bloody last battle of Armageddon takes place. The judgment is completed. The new heaven and new earth are installed, and the new Jerusalem descends from above. God's power is unleashed in righteous violence over the world, bringing judgment and justice to the world. In this reading, then, Revelation undercuts the contrast between godly power and worldly power. Indeed, it is God using worldly, violent "power over" as I have defined it.

But scholars like Loren Johns, Michael Gorman, and Richard Bauckham show a sharp contrast between two powers running through the book of Revelation.[22] Jesus rules as the Lamb who was slain. He sits at the right hand of the throne of God. From this throne, He shall eventually bring the new heavens and new earth, where there shall be no more tears (Rev. 21:1–4). Babylon, however, rules with the worldly power of empire. It brings destruction (Rev. 18). Revelation's challenge to Christians is to be faithful to the way of the Lamb through the trials and sufferings in this world, for God's power shall surely overcome.

After the opening vision of Jesus and the messages to the seven churches, the book turns to reveal the throne of God. John weeps before the throne, asking, "Who is worthy to open the scroll and break its seals?" (Rev. 5:2). Who is worthy to set into motion the judgment and final consummation of history? One of the elders around the throne says, "Do not weep. See, the Lion of the tribe of Judah, the Root of David, has conquered," and He shall open the seals (v. 5). And so a messianic lion, full of power, will surely appear and lead the struggle for victory over evil. But in stunning fashion, a Lamb appears, "standing as if it had been slaughtered" (v. 6). As all the elders gather around, recounting the sacrifice of Jesus taking in the violence and sin of the world, they sing, "Worthy is the Lamb that was slaughtered to receive power and wealth and wisdom and might and honor and glory and blessing" (v. 12). The image paints history as that which shall be ruled by the way of the Lamb, not empire; by godly power, not worldly power; and we must be faithful to Him till the end.[23]

The narration moves on to chapters 6 through 20. Multiple waves of God's judgment sweep over Babylon. The grandiose imagery, so typical of apocalyptic literature, depicts war and violence. But all of this must be interpreted as apocalyptic imagery. It cannot be forgotten that it is still the Lamb, with the signs of "being slaughtered" still on His body, who shall bring in His kingdom. As scholar John Yeatts says so persua-sively, the series of six judgments, unleashed by the seals, portrays "the inevitable progression in a world that trusts in military solutions to problems. The point is that war leads to civil strife, which in turn leads to material deprivation and finally to death."[24] Worldly power brings death, not God. But the Lamb of God, who was slain, who stands at the center of this narrative, brings in His kingdom of life via suffering, presence, and love.

And so Revelation brings us to the final, cataclysmic battle scene, the final victory of righteousness and judgment over the evil in chapter 19. As Michael Gorman notes, on at least five occasions preparations for a final battle are made in Revelation. The last is in chapter 19, where Christ appears on a white horse. His robe is marked by His own blood, not that of the enemies. And Gorman says, "At this battle, as in all the other battles, however, *no actual fighting occurs!* . . . We learn the fate of the enemies of God, but this is more a battle summary or report of the casualties (e.g., Rev. 19:20–21). . . . There is no actual final battle in Revelation."[25] The images of the battle should not be read literally. As throughout the rest of the book, they are images to communicate a reality. In this case they proclaim the reality of God's defeat of evil, not the means of the defeat.[26] Instead, it is the Lamb who was slain who rids the world of evil. He does so not with a sword in His hand to literally shed the blood of His enemies. Instead, "with only his own blood and a sword in his mouth (19:15)," He wins the final battle, via the power of His proclaimed Word and the convicting work of the Spirit.[27] And so two powers are at work in the world, not one. And it is godly power that shall bring in His kingdom.

The final scene, the new Jerusalem, is this place of the eternal power and presence of God, where there shall be no more tears, no more death. God's power is present, but He does not rule "over" humanity in this place. He dwells fully among humanity by His presence. And here there is no more need for the temple (Rev. 21:22), for He fully dwells with humanity. The power of the world has been vanquished. The rule of God, by godly power, as led by the Lamb of God, has been restored for all to live and dwell with God forever.

All Authority Is Given to Me

Right before Jesus ascends to the right hand of the Father, He commissions His disciples with the famous words: "All authority in heaven and on earth has been given to me" (Matt. 28:18). It is a stunning, all-encompassing statement of Jesus's authority over the world (in heaven and on earth) as the mission of God commences into the world. The apostles are sent with the words, "Go therefore and make disciples" (v. 19), to live this call "under" this newly founded authority of Jesus. He promises, "I am with you always, to the end of the age" (v. 20). And so Jesus sets the terms of the flourishing of this new mission. His disciples shall live "under" His authority in all they do in His name. And as they do, He will be "with" them, His presence and power at work among them. It is all a description of how godly power shall work among His disciples as they come "under" His power, making possible the manifestation of His power "with" them. As was said earlier, true "power with" is made possible where we give up "power over" in order to be "under God's power." Jesus's person and work have inaugurated this power.

There are two words most often used to describe "power" in the New Testament. One is the Greek word *dynamis* (used 117 times), most often translated as "power," and the other is *exousia* (used 113 times), most often translated as "authority." These words, often confused, have a long history in sociology as well as New Testament studies.[28] There is much overlap between the two words, but *dynamis* seems most often to accompany the supernatural, miracles, events, and actions not controlled by human means, while *exousia* seems to represent the delegation of power, assigned, given, authorized for humans to act out of.[29]

Dynamis, for example, is released via Jesus and His ministry, as when Luke records that "the power of the Lord was with [Jesus] to heal" (Luke 5:17). *Dynamis* goes out from Him and heals all (Luke 6:19; cf. Mark 5:27–30). His miracles throughout the Gospels are designated *dynameis*, activities of power, demonstrations of power over death, evil, and demons (e.g., Matt. 11:20–23). Mark 6:5–6 tells us that Jesus "could do no deed of power [*dynamis*] there, except that he laid his hands on a few sick people and cured them. And he was amazed at their unbelief." There is this sense that this power is set loose from the hand of God by the Spirit through Jesus, but it is a power that flows out from Him, beyond His immediate purview, dependent upon people trusting Him, making space for His power to work.

And yet Jesus released this power repeatedly within a given authority (*exousia*). He is accused of usurping God's *exousia* when He forgives sins and heals the paralytic (Luke 5:17–26). But Jesus makes clear this authority has been given Him from God the Father. He is living in constant submission to the Father (22:42).[30] And so when Jesus Himself receives all authority in heaven and earth (Matt. 28:18), and He reigns in authority over the world until all enemies have been made subject (1 Cor. 15:25), He, now seated at the right hand of God, becomes the source of all authority. He now delegates authority to His servants. In and under this authority, the dynamic power of God, as released in Jesus by the Spirit, operates on terms different from those on which worldly power operates. It is a power that heals, convicts, reconciles, restores, transforms, and can be set loose only under one's submission to the *exousia* of Jesus, the one who now reigns. It cannot be controlled, only authorized.[31]

This is seen throughout the rest of the New Testament. The gifts of the Spirit possess the authority of the Spirit as given, delegated, authorized by the Lord Himself, who gives the gifts from the seat of His rule (Eph. 4:8–9), always "for building up the body" (v. 12), never for one's self-aggrandizement. As we have already seen, Paul gives up all as loss so that he might be found "in him," under His authority, that he "might know Christ and the power [*dynamis*] of his resurrection" (Phil. 3:8–10). The dynamic power of God in Christ is released only in cruciformity, humility, and weakness, as we come under the authority of the Lord at work among us. This is how "under power" works.

This is the way God's power works in the new era of His kingdom begun in the reign of Jesus. There is worldly authority, which humans control, and godly power, which only God controls. And all who enter into His kingdom are called to live in submission to Christ, under His authority, resisting worldly power, becoming a conduit for His power. We submit to the reign and authority of Christ (*exousia*), and as we do, His healing, transformative, godly power (*dynamis*) is released among us, never in our own control, only submitted to and cooperated with.

A Lost World

I return to this chapter's opening story. George could not imagine power working in any other way but "power over." He was wary of me disavowing power over, because I carried it in the room no matter if I acknowledged it or not. But I was (and still am) convinced that the power of God is released when I give up that worldly power, refuse it, and submit to others in mutuality, releasing the power and presence of Jesus among us.

And yet this power, released "under" and in submission to Jesus, is still power. As in John 20, Jesus sends the disciples out in this power as the Father has sent Him, in humble submission to the authority of God the Father (v. 21). But He sends them out with the power of the Spirit to forgive sins and retain sins (vv. 22–23). As in Luke 10, Jesus sends the disciples out with authority to break the chains of sin and death and of Satan himself (10:17–19). But these same disciples are not to claim this power as their own. Instead, they are to rejoice that they are participants in the kingdom, their very names "written in heaven" (v. 20). This is the way the power of the kingdom of Christ works.

The church of North America, much like George, often lacks imagination for such power. We rarely make space for the living God to work among us in His power. Likewise, the culture around us (in the West) cannot imagine a power that changes the world without coercion, that can get anything done without the human control of power. The sense of God's power, active and at work among us, has been lost amid the fray of our busyness and the outrage our world feels at all the new revealings of injustice amplifying around us.

And so we live in a one-dimensional world where there is only one power, not two. And this power is "power over" in all its various versions used to accomplish the most minimal of change for the good of our world.[32] Faced with grotesque exploitation, hideous wars, and mass shootings, we cannot help but turn to force, anger, and the antagonisms that come with it, to get our agendas done in God's name. We cannot muster the courage, it seems, to be present to God among the suffering. The power of God gets lost, as we blur godly power with worldly power and lose entirely how God would accomplish His purposes in the world.

This problem of blurring the two powers is what we turn to next.

3

The Persistent Temptation to Blur the Powers

> If this plan or this undertaking is of human origin, it will fail; but if it is of God, you will not be able to overthrow them.
>
> Acts 5:38–39

Mars Hill Church in Seattle was once one of the largest evangelical megachurches in North America. It was planted in 1996 by young pastor Mark Driscoll along with Lief Moi and Mike Gunn. It rose to enormous size and influence, and then, amid a series of scandals, it collapsed and folded in 2014. The whole story is told in a podcast series titled "The Rise and Fall of Mars Hill," produced by *Christianity Today*.

At the beginning the church was run by a group of elders "equal in authority," "led by a consensus." Driscoll argues publicly for "removing the concept of the senior pastor" from the church and, instead, empowering other "avenues of leadership and authority." He states, "This is not a dictatorship.

Jesus is our senior pastor." He uses the words "mutually submissive" to describe the leadership of Mars Hill, ridiculing the idea of "CEO pastor." From all accounts, Mars Hill Church was founded on resisting worldly "power over." The leaders intentionally chose a mode of leading "under" godly power, the power of Jesus's presence at work in their midst.[1]

Seven years later, however, a shift happens among the leaders. Driscoll makes a proposal to the existing elder board to appoint a more centralized executive group able to expedite decisions with Driscoll in charge. Some of the elders question the change. The next Sunday, Driscoll gaslights these elders from the pulpit, saying they are holding back the church. After the service, he fires two of the dissenters, "using expletives" and telling them that they can agree to "leave quietly or we'll do an investigation."[2] In contrast to all the commitments they had made previously together, Driscoll forces a change in the leadership structure from a group of persons in mutual submission to godly power, with Jesus at the center, to worldly power, where one man exerts singular power "over" the others via a chain of command.

The next day, after Driscoll has dismissed those two elders, while speaking at a pastors' conference, he says, "Too many guys waste too much time trying to move stiff-necked stubborn and obstinate people. . . . There is a pile of dead bodies behind the Mars Hill bus and by God's grace it will be a mountain by the time we are done. You either get on the bus or you get run over by the bus, those are the options but the bus ain't gonna stop. Yesterday we fired two elders for the first time in the history of Mars Hill last night. They're off the bus. Under the bus. They were off mission so now they're unemployed." Driscoll's understanding of authority and power has changed. He now exercises "power over" people, and in the process he becomes a dictator.

Over the ensuing months, Driscoll's leadership becomes coercive and abusive. A gradual blurring takes place between godly power "with" and worldly power "over." Driscoll takes hold of power "over" in the name of God and His mission. According to Mike Cosper, the podcast narrator, Driscoll begins to reference the increasing church attendance whenever he needs to justify his power moves. The church is growing and it needs a more decisive leadership. He says that we do what we do so people can meet Jesus, not so we can grow big numbers at the church. In the process, he blurs the use of worldly power with the purposes of godly power.

The podcast references how often Driscoll seemed to suggest that if a church stops growing at five thousand, ten thousand, or fifteen thousand, then people will stop being reached for Jesus. So, if you slowed down the church, pumped the brakes on making any decisions, "you were aiding and abetting Satan." You were the anti-Jesus. Using coercive and unilateral "power over" was justified in the name and mission of God. The two powers were explicitly blurred. Soon Driscoll became maniacal, abusive, and even perverse in the way he treated and talked about people. The church of Jesus Christ became the church of Mark Driscoll. And it imploded under the weight of his abuse. And he was disgraced and removed.

It is an all too familiar story. A church leader starts out with a deep sense of trust and dependence upon God. They are surrendered to God, His purposes, His presence as the driver of ministry. They are leading in submission to and in cooperation with the power of God. As a result, people trust them. But, as the ministry flourishes and numbers grow, as is inevitable under God's power, organizing the ministry becomes strained. The struggle to make decisions efficiently takes over. The pastor who once lived "under" God's power begins to exercise increasing control of "power over" under the pretext of getting things done for God. The two powers are blurred. "Power over" takes over in the name of God.

Pretty soon decisions and directives are made "over" people. The leader gets coercive, even abusive, in their use of power. Because worldly power can often get things done within the purposes of God, this all gets ignored. When things go well, the leader is excused in the name of serving God more expediently. The blurring of the two powers gets in motion. Armed with results, the leader becomes intoxicated with power and begins to think subconsciously that they are (acting in the place of) God. A sick narcissism takes hold when "power over" is joined with a "God complex." The leader is beyond accountability. The abuse of persons is justified in the name of God. It is the danger that comes with the blurring of the two powers, and it does incalculable damage to the lives of people who find themselves in its path.

The History of Blurring

The blurring of the two powers is a persistent temptation down through the centuries. The sin of Mark Driscoll has been with us for centuries. It did not suddenly appear in America's contemporary megachurches. It lies at the core of many of the church's most egregious sins down through history, including its alignment with (or assimilation of) racism, slavery, Euro colonialism, White supremacy, and various forms of sexual and spiritual abuse. Whenever the church blurs worldly "power over" with the name of God, abuse regularly follows.

A quick perusal of the church's past, beginning with Jesus again, shows the church's history of back-and-forth struggle between differentiating the two powers and then blurring them all over again.

Jesus

Jesus founded His ministry on His refusal to blur the two powers. I do not need to repeat the account of Jesus's ministry from the previous chapter. Let us just note that Jesus not only differentiated the two powers; He continually resisted the blurring of the two powers. And so the church should continue to do likewise.

All around Jesus, Jews were calling for the use of worldly power to defeat Roman oppression. Palestine was under Roman occupation, and the Romans ruled with brutality. Insurrectionist groups like the Zealots regularly took up violence against Rome in the name of God's reign. And the Jewish people expected that any messiah worthy of the name would do likewise: take up worldly "power over" to establish God's kingdom. Jesus resisted. He refused to blur the two powers.

Like those around them, the disciples expected the new kingdom to begin with coercive force. As they looked toward going to Jerusalem, they believed they'd be confronting the forces of Rome and asked Jesus, "Grant us to sit, one at your right hand and one at your left, in your glory" (Mark 10:37). It is here that Jesus says the "not so among you"! He couldn't have been clearer. There is the power of Rome and there is the power of the kingdom of God. The church shall be founded on the latter, resisting the blurring between the two powers.

At the Last Supper (most likely), Judas (not Iscariot) says to Jesus, "Lord, how is it that you will manifest yourself to us, and not to the world?" (John 14:22 RSV). Judas has no concept of how a king can exercise his power in the world in such a way that it does not display its massive force upon the whole world, so as to be seen by the whole world. And so Jesus responds, "Those who love me will keep my word, and my Father will love them, and we will come to them and make our home with them" (v. 23). In the face of Judas's desire to use worldly "power over," Jesus declares that it shall be through the loving, convicting, relational, powerful presence of God that He shall bring His kingdom.

Jesus's whole life, from the time He rejected Satan's temptation to take up the world's "power over," to His healing of people's diseases and the exorcising of demons in the power of the Spirit, to the Sermon on the Mount's "love your enemies," to His washing the disciples' feet at Passover supper, to His healing of the soldier's ear, to His standing before Pilate, to His submitting to the cross, is one continuous demonstration of Himself being under the power of God. For Jesus there was only one right side of power: the side that is under the power of God released by the Spirit in Him. He refused to blur the two powers.

The Early Church

The earliest churches lived "under" the power of Jesus. He breathed on the first disciples the power of the Spirit, and He sent them out into the world under Her power with the keys of the kingdom (John 20:23). He commanded them, "Stay here in the city until you have been clothed with power from on high" (Luke 24:49). And so Jesus set into motion new community after new community, organizing people under the power of God manifested in the presence of the risen Christ through the Holy Spirit.

This was not power of the worldly, coercive type. This was the power of the keys of the kingdom—"If you forgive the sins of any, they are forgiven them; if you retain the sins of any, they are retained" (John 20:23). Together, disciples of Jesus everywhere slowly cultivated a "patient ferment" of social life under Christ's power. These communities eventually permeated the whole of the Roman Empire.[3] Early Christian writer Justin Martyr described these new Christians as saying, "We who once murdered each other indeed no longer wage war against our enemies; moreover, so as not to bear false witness before our interrogators, we cheerfully die confessing Christ."[4]

A century later, Christian teacher Origen challenged the Caesarean Christians of his time not to blur the powers. "For you who are redeemed by Christ . . . a physical sword has been removed from your hands. . . . In its place the 'sword of the Spirit' has been given and you must seize it." For Origen, Christians are to fight the evil powers by means of "prayers and fasts, justice and piety, gentleness, chastity and all the virtues of self control." "One saint who prays is much more powerful than countless sinners who wage war." Origen, as one voice among many, urged the Christians of the early church to live under godly power with prayer as their spiritual weapon.[5] He was differentiating godly power from the "power over" of the world.

And yet we know that the early church was not a monolithic people who rejected any and all participation in worldly power.[6] As scholar Peter Leithart reminds us, despite all the anecdotal evidence, there was no uniform doctrinal commitment concerning the refusal of violence and military service among the early church communities.[7] There were differences among Christians on using violence in self-defense.

Nonetheless, the pervasive anecdotal evidence from Origen and Justin Martyr, as well as the evidence of church disagreement pointed out by Leithart, shows how much the churches of this time period were grappling with the new realities of godly power released among them under the rule of Jesus. They were figuring out how to differentiate between the two powers and how to live accordingly. The fact that these questions were so regularly discerned suggests just how much the lives of early Christians were being challenged as they sought to live under the godly power of Jesus's presence.[8] They were struggling to resist the blurring of the two powers: the old powers of coercion and the new power of Jesus Christ released among them.

And so, even though at this point they were not organized in such a way as to have policies to refuse "power over," they nonetheless were persistently discerning the two powers and resisting their blurring. They lived under the conviction, in Alan Kreider's words, that "on the cross Jesus had exposed the true nature of the demonic powers and vanquished them . . . and through the Holy Spirit, had unleashed unimaginable spiritual power for good in the world." They lived by prayer, exorcisms, healings, and giving care to the poor, with a patience that refused to coerce.[9]

Constantine

In AD 312, the Roman emperor Constantine became a Christian. On the night before he led his army into the massive Battle of the Milvian Bridge, he had a vision of the Christian God. They won that battle over Maxentius and crossed the Tiber River into Rome, and Constantine became the undisputed emperor of all the Western Empire. He attributed this victory to the Christian God and converted to Christianity soon thereafter.

The next year he met the emperor Licinius in Italy, and together they issued the Edict of Milan (313), which gave all Christians legal status in Rome and protected them from persecution. This began a closer relationship between the Roman emperor and the churches. Whereas before, the churches had been persecuted by Rome, now they were protected and even sponsored. According to Eusebius, the great Christian historian, the "Logos" itself (divine wisdom) was now seen at work in Constantine's monarchy. His rule was a stand-in for God's rule.[10] For others, however, this began "the fall of the church": the alignment of state power with the church, the ultimate blurring of the two powers.[11]

From this point, a gradual change took place in the church's understanding of the way God's power works in the world.[12] Instead of assuming that godly power works differently from worldly power, the church gradually assumed that godly power could work through and with the worldly power of the state. The church was more than happy for the emperor to do its bidding. And worldly power became aligned with, and blurred with, the power of God.

In the ensuing years, Constantine would take a role in resolving doctrinal disagreements that sprang up among the churches across the empire. Instead of local churches working these things out in mutuality, as part of everyday life, Constantine would now call a council to solve these disagreements.

The Council of Nicaea gathered in 325 to discern conflicts over Christology and the Son's relation to the Father. Jesus of Nazareth was determined to be divine "in substance" according to Greek metaphysics. Jesus became separated from His history in the people of Israel. The council determined the date of the resurrection and decided when Easter would be celebrated according to the Roman calendar instead of the Jewish calendar and its determination of Passover. It all spoke of a new way of being a Christian. Christianity became aligned with Rome, and godly power became assimilated with the worldly power of Rome and became comfortable with the blurring of the two powers.

Constantine soon would use force—"power over"—to root out heresy. Roman law moved from tolerance of Christians and other faiths to compulsion of one true faith.[13] The discipleship of non-Christians moved from a relational process within each local church to a governing national body. Belief became universalized and enforced by Rome, and a door was opened for what some have labeled supersessionism.[14] Versus being a movement of people extended from God's own historical people Israel, Christianity became a universal faith to be imposed on the whole world from Rome. The road was paved for eventual colonialism.

Those who see this moment as "the fall of the church" see a pattern beginning of the blurring of the two powers.[15] From that point, from the persecutions of the Donatists in the late fourth and fifth centuries, to the brutality of Charlemagne's campaign to convert the Saxons in the late eighth century, to the Crusades and the Spanish Inquisition, all the way to the multiple forms of Euro colonialism in the ensuing centuries, the church gave in to the temptation to use worldly power in the name of God's purposes. The church regularly took the wrong side of power.

We may be sure that God in all His sovereignty was still able to work among the churches throughout this history. With each outbreak of brutality there were still Christians pointing the church toward a return to the way of Jesus and His reign. As historian John Dickson reminds us, there have been many bullies and saints down through the last two thousand years of Christianity, and God has used the saints mightily in the face of the brutes.[16]

But in many ways the stage was set by Constantine. The bad habits of blurring the two powers were set into motion. Hundreds of years later the horrific abuses of colonialism, enslavement of humans, exclusion of women from ministry, and bad missionary practices would follow in the name of God. It shows the horror that happens whenever the church blurs the two powers and takes up the wrong side of power.

Augustine: The Two Cities

Constantinian Rome fell into disarray in the fifth century. In 410 Germanic tribes sacked Rome. Many attacks later, the Roman emperor was removed. No Roman emperor would rule the "eternal city" again after 476. It was a dumpster fire, and many Romans blamed Rome's fall on its allegiance to the Christian God, who had failed to protect it. The very worldly power that the church had become so comfortable with in the name of God was now in question. Where was God during the attacks? Did He not have power? How did God rule? What was His relationship with the worldly power of Rome?

It was into this mess that the great theologian Augustine wrote his *City of God*, clarifying once again that there are two ways that things work in the world, one via worldly "power over" and the other through God's "power with," and they are entirely different and should never be confused.

Augustine's main theme in the book was not power per se. It was that there are two cities gathered by two different forms of worship. In the one city (of God) desires are ordered toward God and the pursuit of His glory, while in the other city (of man) desires are ordered toward the self and the pursuit of fleshly desire (14.1 4). Ultimately the two cities are distinguished by their loves (19.24–26). The city of God loves God even to the contempt of self; the other city loves self even to the contempt of God (14.28).

But power does come into play in all of this. For as surely as the earthly city lives by the flesh, the power of human coercion and human effort must be its means. And as surely as the city of God lives unto the glory of God, the power of the Holy Spirit will rule in that city (14.1–4).

Faced with the downfall of Rome, Augustine distinguishes two different ways of living in response to it. One way is to live through worldly power; the other is to live under the power of God. The two cities, two ways of living, will coexist side by side. Eventually one city (of God) will overtake the other (of man). In the meantime, the two cities, with two ways of life and two very different kinds of power at work, live side by side. And they must remain unblurred.

For sure there will be times when the people of God will exercise the worldly power of government in ways more fortunate for the people under that rule. But this way will still "lack the perfection of righteousness" possible in the city of God.[17] For sure there will be the temptation to blur the powers, and so, for Augustine, there must be an invisible, true church faithful to God and His glory. This true church of the city of God will live among the visible, earthly city and its ways of worldly power. But for Augustine, people should not and cannot live in both cities simultaneously.[18] People must choose between the two cities. The power, and the loves, must remain unblurred.

Eventually, however, even Augustine, as bishop of Hippo, succumbed to the blurring of the two powers. He recommended the use of military force to coerce the Donatists, accused of heresy, to obey the righteous decisions of the councils. Augustine, who himself testified to the need to remain vigilant in distinguishing the two powers, found himself on the wrong side of power.

Luther: The Right Hand and the Left Hand

Several hundred years later, the Great Peasants' Revolt (1524–25) was erupting in Europe. The Holy Roman Empire, having become a piecemeal group of kingdoms and magistrates theoretically under the one rule of the pope, was disintegrating. Martin Luther, that Catholic monk, was protesting the corruption of the Roman church and its use of worldly "power over" people. He railed against the church's use of "indulgences" to coerce people into giving money. He denounced the church's corrupt hierarchies and called for the church to affirm the "priesthood of all believers." And a riot broke out. Massive numbers of peasants revolted against the nobility and the oppressive class system of medieval Europe.

Though Luther sympathized with the peasants and the unjust conditions of their lives, the violence of the mobs threatened anarchy, and Luther's views took a quick right turn. He wrote *Against the Murderous, Thieving Hoards of Peasants*, in which he urged the German nobles to strike down the peasants as one would kill a mad dog. Luther was able to do this by distinguishing between the two powers. Worldly power, Luther thought, had to keep the good order of society, so that God's power could tend to the work of saving souls.

A few years earlier, Luther had clarified the role of two powers in his *Temporal Authority: To What Extent It Should Be Obeyed*. For Luther, one power (or estate or government) was temporal and restrained the unchristian and wicked so that they were obliged to keep their lives orderly; this power maintained an outward peace. Government may use the power of the sword to this end. Luther called this God's left hand. The other power was spiritual and shaped Christian souls unto sanctification and righteousness. This was a work of the Holy Spirit, and Luther called this power God's right hand. Luther affirmed: there are two powers, not one. They are starkly different: the one rules by coercion, force, and "power over"; the other by love, the Spirit, and redemption.[19] And under no circumstances should they be confused.[20]

And so once again we have a church resisting the blurring of the two powers. But notice: the work of ordering the social world was the work of God's left hand, worldly "power over," and this power would preserve society, nothing more. The right hand of God's saving power would save and sanctify souls for holy living. This would become the basis of Luther's two-kingdom theology. In the centuries to follow, this theology would shape a worldview that segregated the two powers, so that the power of the Spirit, godly power, would be located solely in the redemption of souls. God's noncoercive power would now have nothing to do with the work of God's justice in society. For this, then, we must now rely on worldly power.

Many historians today attribute the capitulation of Luther's German people to Hitler in the 1930s to this development of the two-kingdoms approach to power. For German Lutherans, church and government operate via the two different powers, godly power and worldly power. The government was to operate in total autonomy, independent of the church, in the work of ordering society (*Eigengesetzlichkeit*). The church was to submit to government in social matters (Rom. 13) and stick to taking care of souls. This account of Germany can surely be debated.[21] Nonetheless, we see the danger of sequestering godly power of the Spirit to the interior of the soul, allowing the government to do what it must do in the ordering of the social world.[22]

Today we see this view of the two powers lingering among American Protestants. When evangelicals pursue government to do God's work in protecting a Christian culture, or when mainline Protestants pursue government alone to do the work of social justice, we see this view of the two powers at work. In the process, Christians push aside the work of godly power to heal, restore, and renew our society.

And so, strangely, distinguishing the two powers in the Lutheran way leads to an unintentional blurring of the two powers all over again. Since we cannot expect God's redemptive power (Luther's right hand) to be at work in the world, we are left with only worldly "power over" to manage evil (Luther's left hand), preserve society, and achieve justice in the world. Because now only one power, worldly "power over," is all we have left to do justice in the world, we who seek God's justice in the world are forced to use worldly "power over" to do God's work. We are forced to blur worldly power with God's purposes for justice in the world. We have no choice but to be on the wrong side of power.

Niebuhr and Christian Realism

Moving into the modern era, we find Reinhold Niebuhr, a towering figure of American public theology of the last century, accusing Luther of setting the stage for the German church's "quietism" in the face of the Nazi evil in the 1930s. For Niebuhr, Luther's two-kingdoms theology trained the church to leave the government alone to do its business, while the church stuck to its knitting, taking care of souls. It was an ideology that allowed the German church to opt out of engaging the Nazi state on its gross injustices.[23] Faced with the horrors of Hitler, Niebuhr proposed an alternative approach.

Niebuhr said Christians have to be "realistic" about the world, humanity, sin, and power. Humans are born into the sinful world with the limits of fleshly existence and the givenness of power struggles. Because we humans can see beyond ourselves (we are "transcendent"), we are prone to self-centeredness, egoism, selfishness, and pride.[24] We are tempted to "play God"—the original sin of Genesis 3:22—to use power overzealously to achieve what we see as God's righteousness.

For Niebuhr, this meant that we humans can aspire individually to overcome our selfishness through Jesus. But when selfish people get together in groups, those "self-regarding impulses" are compounded.[25] And Jesus cannot help solve these problems of politics. Politics and societal problems need worldly power to put them in order. The ethic of Jesus "has nothing to say about the relativities of politics and economics, nor of the necessary balances of power which exist and must exist in even the most intimate social relationships."[26] For Niebuhr, Jesus, with all His power, is impotent for engaging the injustices at work in the modern world.

For Niebuhr, then, worldly "power over" is a given of our sinful human social existence. It is the only power at work in society. It helps keep the world in order. We cannot live without it.

And justice can be achieved only "through a system of checks and balances that preserves unto each group a measure of power sufficient to weigh effectively against that of any other group by which it might be maltreated."[27] Over against the unrealistic optimism of Protestant social liberalism, Niebuhr challenged Christians to get real and practical toward using power to achieve proximate justice in a sinful world. Let us do it in the name of Jesus and His love, which inspires us to be just. This came to be known as Niebuhr's "Christian realism." It is the modern-day version of what I have termed the standard account of power.

This too, however, is still a version of the blurring of the two powers. As happened with versions of Luther's two-kingdoms theology, the power of Jesus gets sequestered off to the work in the soul of the individual alone. As we go into the world, however, there is only one power left: worldly power. If the Christian is to use any power in the world, he or she must use worldly "power over" to do the work for a proximate justice, the best justice we can hope for in a sinful world. According to Niebuhr, we should do this in the name of Jesus's love.

This is the Niebuhrian effect. Under the influence of Reinhold Niebuhr and his brother, H. Richard, it affects much of Christianity today. Jesus's power is for the soul. The work of managing culture for justice is the domain of worldly "power over" only.[28] Removing Jesus's power from the work of justice leaves only one power to do the work of God.[29] The two powers are blurred into one by elimination.

We Are All Niebuhrians Now

The Niebuhrian effect pervades today's evangelicals and Protestants in general. It is evident when a social activist limits God's work of justice to only what can be accomplished through the government or capitalist funding ventures. It is evident when churches seek to impact culture for God's morality by getting a Christian elected to Congress or putting Christians in positions of power at influential cultural institutions.[30] It is evident when Mark Driscoll insists that practicality and urgency require that he take "over" making unilateral decisions more efficiently for Mars Hill Church. Basically, Christians everywhere are Niebuhrians now.

When Christians see power only in terms of the one power given in the world, they in essence blur the powers. God's power and purposes get blurred with worldly, coercive "power over." We think if we refuse to use this "power over" in the world, we in essence are forfeiting engaging at all with the world and its injustice. We have no imagination for how God's power, unleashed in Jesus, by the Spirit, is working in the world for justice and healing. When it comes to justice, we are left therefore with no choice but to take the side of worldly power on God's behalf. We are doomed to work on the wrong side of power.[31]

The rise of evangelicalism's alignment with Donald Trump, with the rise of the so-called Christian nationalism movement, comes from this side of power. It is to this story we now turn.

4

The Lure of Christian Nationalism

The Refusal of God's Power

> All who exalt themselves will be humbled, and all who humble themselves will be exalted.
>
> Matthew 23:12

> For you say, "I am rich, I have prospered, and I need nothing."
>
> Revelation 3:17

On a cold Saturday afternoon in January of 2016, people gathered at the Dordt College chapel in Sioux Center, Iowa, to hear the new front-runner for the Republican nomination for president. Dordt College, a conservative Reformed Christian college, was hosting Donald Trump. He gave a stunner of a sixty-seven-minute speech that would become infamous across the nation's cable news outlets. The speech set the stage for Trump's eventual victorious 2016 presidential campaign.

Trump preached to the crowd. "I will tell you, Christianity is under tremendous siege, whether we want to talk about it or we don't want to talk about it," he said. According to his statistics, Christians made up an overwhelming majority of the country, "and yet we don't exert the power that we should have." Trump promised that if he were elected president, things would change. He gestured to the crowd, waving his index finger, promising, "Christianity will have power. If I'm there, you're going to have plenty of power, you don't need anybody else. You're going to have somebody representing you very, very well. Remember that." Trump's words are telling. If Christians voted for Trump, they would have power, they wouldn't need anyone else? Even Jesus?

Trump may have lost the Iowa caucus that following week, but, as Elizabeth Dias of the *New York Times* detailed, Trump galvanized evangelical White Christians over the ensuing months all over America. A vast majority of them, including the ones there in Iowa, turned out to vote for him. They came to see Trump as their protector, as the one who would keep them safe.[1] Feeling like the culture all around them was closing in on them, this group of Christians had tired of their concerns being dismissed, ignored, or ridiculed by the perceived elites of the culture. So they elected Trump as someone who would exert power on their behalf, the cause of Christ, as they saw it.

Trump was the revealing of a theology of power at work in those evangelicals who voted for him in 2016. This theology urges Christians to take up worldly power in the name of God, on behalf of God, for the purposes of God. And while White evangelicals were roundly criticized for voting for a man with racist, non-Christian policies toward immigration, or for voting for a misogynist, sexist man, no one, to my knowledge, fully challenged the theology of power at work in evangelicals voting for Trump. There were many who correctly saw a reversion to White racism being played out. But no one saw the evangelical alignment with Trump as a rejection of the Holy Spirit's work for justice in our schools, our town halls, our hospitals, and so on.

It is of course the well-worn theology that permeates American Christianity, both evangelical and mainline. It advocates that Christians work aggressively to control worldly power to accomplish God's purposes. It is the blurring of the powers. It is the unexamined assumption that drives our politics. It is the Niebuhrian way. We assume, on both the conservative and liberal sides of church in America, that this is what we are supposed to do as Christians with our politics.

But each time it wreaks destruction in its path. Pastors become narcissists. Leaders become ogres. Sunday school teachers become sexual predators. And when we gain control of the White House and foist Christian morality upon American culture, America becomes less Christian, not more.

It is as if each time worldly power gets blurred with God's power, the very metaphysics of worldly power changes. "Power over" (the definition of worldly power) gets unhinged from any restraints (because surely no one should stand in the way of God). And the sin of usurping God, and using worldly power in the name of God, becomes the open door to wanton abuse. We've seen it with abusive pastors, we've seen it with Driscoll, we've seen it with Trump and his Christian followers, we've seen it on January 6 at the US Capitol, we've seen it at play in churches all over the country. It is the corrupting sin at the core of our lives. It is the corrupting sin at the core of the fall of evangelicalism in the twenty-first century.

And Yet We Still Need It

And yet we cannot just get rid of worldly power entirely. It's not that easy. God's power, in Jesus, by the Holy Spirit, at work in the world, requires the cooperation of people. God will not coerce. And so we must be careful not to disavow all use of all worldly power for the work of justice. There are times when worldly power must do some work to preserve a society. And so worldly power is still needed by Christians in the world because we cannot assume that those around us will make space for God's power.

The argument, for many of those Christians in Iowa who supported Trump for president, was that we need worldly power to preserve our freedoms from a culture encroaching upon us with its anti-Christian demands. We can no longer teach our children the ways of God when it comes to sexuality and gender, marriage and the Bible, in the public schools. We are being ordered to support same-sex marriages even when it is against our religious convictions. We need someone to protect our freedoms so we can live out our convictions even if others despise us.

There is something to this argument. Putting aside disagreements over the moral commitments of the Iowan Christians, the coercive powers of government can be used positively to preserve a society from conflictual violence, disorganized chaos, and one people group's abusive treatment of another. Worldly power via hierarchical structures, payrolls, and court systems can run businesses when the people who do business with each other and who have conflicts are not mutually submitted to the reign of Jesus. In these cases, lawyers may come in handy. In the world, we should expect, there will be times when Christians have no choice but to use worldly power. It will be a constant navigation: Christians will have to discern when and how to use worldly power and when we can make space for God's power to work among us.

For example, Jane, a hospital administrator and medical doctor in a major city, had to discern worldly power in her job almost daily. She sought to organize obstetric care for her city so that lower-income households could afford it. At the same time, she struggled to keep her hospital out of bankruptcy due to lawsuits against the doctors. She had to use legal worldly power against and over certain people who would put her hospital out of business. She could not eschew worldly power, or her hospital, and all its care, would go under.

The doctors of her hospital wanted and expected big salaries. Despite her best efforts relationally, she could not convince the medical professionals to take a pay cut so they could offer the poorer members of the community health care for giving births. Meanwhile, the lawyers were responding to the lawsuits. They insisted that all women giving birth, regardless of their health, be treated as high-risk pregnancies. As a result, the cost for such birth care became five times the cost for a normal delivery of a baby with no complications. This high-cost pregnancy care enabled doctors to make more and more money, as most of the births at the hospital were non-eventful and yet the mothers were charged the price of high-risk pregnancy care anyway. Once compensated at this level, none of the doctors dared give up that money. But now only those citizens with the best healthcare insurance could afford this care.

Jane had to manage as best she could with "power over." She pushed and pulled, trying to hold costs down, motivating doctors toward righteousness, and keeping a healthcare system functioning as best she could for the most people. It was worldly power that kept the system going for some, achieving some good outcomes, but managing to achieve only a minimal amount of justice.

Jane eventually turned to an alternative approach. She gathered some doctors she knew through her church and other organizations. They opened a birth care center in a house near the hospital in the city. Here she offered superior birth care for pregnancies that carried no high risks for one-fifth of what was the cost at the corporate hospital. Her doctors would still make a very good salary but not exorbitant. If a mother developed a high-risk pregnancy, they would quickly move her to the nearby hospital, where care for high-risk pregnancies was available. In the process of all this, space was opened for relationship, care, and much blessing. And out of these birth care spaces the churches ministered to other needs as well. Corporate hospitals, meanwhile, were challenged by the existence of these birth centers. Their excesses were exposed. Health care was called to account for its outrageous greed. Kingdom transformation happened over several years in multiple different ways.

God's power works where persons and institutions make space for Him, discern His working, and cooperate with Him at work in the world. Here the Holy Spirit, through Her relational engaging and loving power, works to heal, disrupt, and even transform. Where there is no space for God, however, God will not impose. This all-powerful God, as revealed in Christ, will not coerce anyone with His power. By His nature, He is love. He works in and among noncoercive relational space.

And so we will need worldly power to organize life for those who do not yet recognize the Holy Spirit's working among their lives, their work, their social organizations. In these places, worldly power will manage institutions in limited ways. But this power cannot heal or restore. And it will need to be held to account, much like those birth centers held the corporate hospitals to account. Worldly power must be kept within its lane. It cannot usurp God and impose restoration and healing on people. It must be ordered within the confines of the sovereignty and lordship of Christ, or it will destroy. Godly power, and what God can do, must be kept separate from worldly power, and what it can do, under the sovereignty of God.

The hospitals of Jane's city were maintaining obstetric services at a high cost. They were delivering services, motivated by money (worldly power), yet still preserving lives, albeit via a high cost. The birthing homes, started by Jane, were also maintaining obstetric services but at a lower cost. And in the birthing homes, under godly power, so much more was happening for healing and renewal beyond the cheaper obstetric services offered. Spaces were being opened for God to work, heal, rearrange lives, and even disrupt the hospitals running on worldly power.

Keeping Worldly Power in Its Lane

Worldly power, at its best, can preserve society, which in itself is a work of justice. But it cannot do God's work of healing, redemption, sanctification, and justice of a deeper kind. The salvific work of God, both personally and socially, is the direct work of God through His transforming power in relational spaces open to Him.[2]

Worldly power functions like a well-placed traffic light at a busy intersection. It keeps cars from crashing into each other and injuring people. Police enforce compliance with the traffic light. If you "run a light," a police officer will stop you and give you a ticket. If this happens too many times, you will be arrested and required to go to court, and you may even have your driver's license revoked. With this kind of coercion and these rules, the traffic light keeps good order and keeps traffic accidents to a minimum.

But traffic lights cannot resolve people's conflicts. They (and the legislative system that enforces them) cannot reconcile those who hate each other or heal the brokenness that may be revealed when two cars come together at an intersection and refuse to yield to one another. Perhaps we would not even need traffic lights if all drivers were patient, loving, and courteous with one another. But the fact that many people run through traffic lights, disregard them, or honk loudly when someone doesn't respond to a green light fast enough reveals the need in our fallen world for traffic lights.

First Timothy 1:9 says, "The law is laid down not for the innocent but for the lawless and disobedient, for the godless and sinful, for the unholy and profane, for those who kill their father or mother, for murderers." But the traffic light will not heal those people of the antagonisms that drive their lives. All worldly power can do is preserve society from the chaos of sin and hold back the forces of evil, so that human life may carry on with its daily tasks. Worldly power therefore must be kept in its lane. We must not try to heal the world through traffic lights.

Martin Luther argued fiercely against worldly power ever crossing over to do God's work.[3] In his 1523 pamphlet *Temporal Authority*, he distinguished between what the two powers can do. He defines worldly power (temporal government) as that which "restrains the unchristian and wicked . . . [in order to] maintain an outward peace." God, however, works salvation through faith, and "faith is a free act, to which no one can be coerced." God must heal and restore through spiritual power. According to Luther, the Christian person, living in the Spirit, has no need for temporal government (the left hand of God), but until that time when all humanity is under the sway of the Spirit, worldly power (as I have defined it) will be needed to hold back the chaos, to allow

the Spirit to do Her work without coercion in the lives of
people.

Modern Reformed theologians argue likewise for a distinction of purposes between worldly power and godly
power.[4] A key issue for these Protestants has been whether
the worldly powers of government (and perhaps other institutions like marriage or economy too) were created before
the fall and thus intended from the beginning for the "good
work" of God (i.e., orders of creation) or whether indeed they
were interventions by God after the fall to hold back sin and
keep human life in order (i.e., orders of preservation).[5] If government was instituted after the fall, then its purpose must
be limited to holding back sin. If government was created
before the fall, then its purposes must be restored to their
original created intent. With the latter, Christians can be
tempted to take over the government for perceived Christian purposes.[6]

In either case, however, we are now living in the world
after the fall. Whether traffic lights were created before the
fall or after the fall, needed because of sin or not, we are now
in a world of sin. It is not possible to live in a world without
traffic lights, even if maybe we could have before the fall. We
need traffic lights to do their work, but only God in Christ
can overcome sin and evil and reveal what and how government (or traffic lights) might be used (or not used) within the
purposes of God. And so as Christians we should never confuse the two powers and what they can do. We should never
yield to the temptation to use worldly power (the government) for God's redemptive purposes. We must be vigilant to
distinguish between worldly power, working via institutions
apart from Christ, and godly power, at work in and through
the church.

The words of Romans 13:1, then—"Let every person be
subject to the governing authorities; for there is no authority

except from God, and those authorities that exist have been instituted by God"—must be read very carefully. This verse should not be read to say that God's *redemptive* purposes are accomplished by the authorities through worldly power. Neither should it be read to endorse a particular government as from God, whether it be that of the murderous Nero (whom some date to the time of this text) or of the hideous Hitler of 1930s Germany. Rather, it is these "authorities" that are always being ordered ("instituted") by God to be kept within their limitations. To be subject to them is to submit to the ordering of these institutions within the very limited purposes they serve under God's sovereign care (Rom. 13:11). To be subject to them is to submit to God and His ordering of them. Romans 13 is a clarion call to keep worldly power in its place.[7]

One of the reasons those evangelicals in Iowa, and other places, voted for Donald Trump was the promise Trump gave them that he would install judges that would overthrow *Roe v. Wade*.[8] For these evangelicals, abortion was murder, and we therefore must protect the most vulnerable among us, the unborn children. But is such law making a preservative action or a salvific one, something only God can do through His noncoercive power?

This is the discerning task of the local church. Is preventing abortion a preservative function of government, to be imposed legislatively? Or is it a work needing the transformative power of God in people's sexual lives, a power that cannot be imposed? Can someone who is not a Christian even see abortion as evil apart from the redemptive, restorative, relational sexual ethic made possible in Christ? If not, then we are forcing people to be Christians in their sexual lives without Jesus, and this goes against the way God works for redemption. There's an argument to be made here on both sides. The church must discern carefully, locally, how to engage those who are pregnant but lack the means or will to be parents. Because once we attempt to do with worldly power what only God can do by His power, we end up on the wrong side of power, and a whole lot can go hideously wrong.

The case of the church and abortion illustrates the necessity of Christian discernment as related to power. Is this a preservative work or a redemptive work? We can align ourselves with worldly power for preservative purposes. But does the situation before us demand that we be present to persons in distress—pregnant women who have no financial or social support to raise a child—and make space for (a witness to) God's power to work among us to redeem and restore, from which we can then cooperate?

When Worldly Power Becomes Unhinged

Something akin to demon-possession happens to worldly power when it becomes blurred with godly power. It's very constitution changes. This is the dark side of the wrong side of power.

Since you cannot put limits on God, when you align worldly power with God's name, it can become unhinged from any limits. Violence is sure to follow. And abuse is sure to follow the violence. The church is prone to this mistake more than any other place, because everything we do in the church is in the name of God. So when we take up worldly power in the church, it can go off the rails like nowhere else.

A presidential candidate in 2020, Andrew Yang, in an article written for *Politico Magazine*, described the intoxication with worldly power that he experienced while running for president. The amount of attention put on him was jarring, and it started to change his view of himself. He described it as the "hubris syndrome," a well-researched psychological disorder that happens to those in "possession of power held over years and with minimal constraint on the leader." Yang, describing medical research, states that neural processes shape the brains of people in specific ways when they occupy seats of power. Such leaders grow in contempt for others and lose the capacity for empathy. Power is "a sort of tumor," he says, citing historian Henry Adams, and it grows and takes over your life. This is what was happening to Yang in the process of running for president of the United States. Ironically, he argues that this is the opposite of the kind of leaders we need in government. I would suggest that the same is true for the church, only worse, because the claim to exercise worldly power on behalf of God in the church happens endemically and emboldens the "hubris syndrome" all the more.[9]

In the famous words of Lord Acton, "Power tends to corrupt and absolute power corrupts absolutely." Acton wrote those words to his professor friend Mandell Creighton, criticizing Creighton's overly charitable view of the Roman Catholic hierarchy. A few sentences later, Acton says, "There is no worse heresy than that the office sanctifies the holder of it."[10] For Acton, giving divine sanction to the one wielding worldly power is a recipe for abuse. That the truth of this statement has endured the test of time speaks for itself. It is testimony to the reality that worldly power, once joined with God's name, leads to hideous abuse.

We all know of leaders who start out well, with the best of intentions, who follow after Jesus with all their heart. They are gracious, loving, and kind, wishing to serve God. But along the way they acquire worldly power through position, fame, or money. In a moment of seizing control of power, as representatives of God, they justify unilateral decisions in the name of God's work. The decisions are enforced via coercion. When something good occurs from it, it feeds the ego. This power then promotes the thought that "I did this" and feeds the ego even more, so that the leaders take even more control. They now think, "I can accomplish good for Jesus through my power." Slowly they become the ultimate decider of the good, breaking through the guardrails that are in place to hold their power in check.

At this point, the exercise of such power puts a person in the position of God, and they thus commit the ultimate sin, the one that poisons the soul (the very first sin in history, identified in Gen. 3:22). It is as if something changes in the constitution of the leader. He or she seems possessed. This corrupting dynamic slowly takes over the person's life and sets the person on a path of horrific evil and disgusting abuse. It all explains how so many good servants of Christ end up going rogue, destroying people in their wake and eventually getting destroyed themselves.

Trump had all these narcissist tendencies before he was ever elected president. He famously said in that Dordt College speech, "I could stand in the middle of Fifth Avenue and shoot somebody, and I wouldn't lose any voters, OK?" Throughout his presidency he believed he was invincible, did not need to read security briefs, did not need to obey the laws that put his power within the guardrails of the constitution. Much ink has been spilled on the narcissism of Donald Trump.

But these are also the traits that possess a person when they exercise worldly power, free from any guardrails, believing they are acting on behalf of God, or, worse, when they believe they are God. This sickness is treacherous and should never infect the church. It should not infect a Christian who exercises worldly power in the world. But it does. And whenever it does, it is a massive failure of the church to discern the wrong side of power, to discern the difference between worldly power and godly power, and it thus allows worldly power to take on the mantle of God.

When the Powers Go Rogue

Institutions and systems, not just individuals, can go rogue. They too can become possessed by worldly power aligned with God's name. The apostle Paul addresses this issue in terms of "the principalities and powers." Paul says these systems—"whether thrones or dominions or rulers or powers"—were "created through [Christ] and for him. . . . In him all things hold together" (Col. 1:15–17). They are not evil in and of themselves. They can do the good work to preserve us.[11] But something happens when these authorities overreach, try to do more than preserve life, go beyond their limits, and act as if they are God in autonomy from Him.

In the words of one Anabaptist theologian, these authorities "did not accept the modesty that would have permitted them to remain conformed to the creative purpose . . . but rather claimed absolute authority."[12] They are now in rebellion. Paul refers to them as *stoicheia*—elements or elemental spirits (Col. 2:8, 20)—and elsewhere he calls them "the ruler of the power of the air, the spirit that is now at work among those who are disobedient," "the cosmic powers of this present darkness," and "the rulers of this age" (Eph. 2:2; 6:12; 1 Cor. 2:6). These rules or laws or authorities that were once meant to guide and preserve our lives have now turned hostile and enslave us into evil.

The apostle Paul describes these powers as if they are possessed by Satan. In their supposed autonomy from God, rejecting any guardrails, these systems go rogue, and domination, abuse, and violence soon follow. Walter Wink says, "The actual spirituality of systems and structures [has] betrayed their divine vocations."[13] These systems have become the enfleshment by which Satan inhabits and oppresses people and works his evil. If we allow ourselves to be swept up into this evil, we will find ourselves enslaved to these powers too (Gal. 4:3).

Once we have gone this direction, the only way these "rulers and authorities" can be dismantled is in the reign of Jesus. Under Christ's power, the spell of their power has already been broken and must be broken. And so we who are in Christ, under His lordship, must stand under His power and refuse the sovereignty of the powers over us (Col. 2:15).[14] The church as a people, together in Christ, must refuse to give these powers a material, systemic reality in which to exercise their evil.

When we see worldly power in these terms, it gives us new understanding of the violence and mayhem on January 6, 2021, at the US Capitol building. It gives new insight into the horrors of a Putin or the ideology of a Nazi Party that took over the German people in the 1930s.[15] It helps us see how easily government, education, and health care, all intended for good, can go rogue. It gives new urgency to the calling of every Christian who enters the world's systems and who would dare exercise worldly power: we must discern carefully any exercise of worldly power that would try to be God and stray from its God-ordered limits. Refuse to blur the powers. Know the limits of worldly power. Keep it in its lane.

Many so-called evangelicals identified the ascendency of Trump with that of the emperor Cyrus, whom God used to free the Jews and return them to the promised land and who is referred to in Isaiah 45 as God's instrument for that purpose. Like Cyrus, Trump was corrupt. But according to Lance Wallnau, Jerry Falwell Jr., Kenneth Copeland, and others, God could still use him to accomplish His purposes. They pushed this apologetic for Trump, especially when his grotesque moral behavior became apparent time and time again and required an apology.

But let us be clear. Even though God in His sovereignty allowed Cyrus to be used within God's purposes, this was not

God endorsing human use of worldly power to somehow redeem the world. According to Isaiah 45:1, God anointed Cyrus "to subdue nations before him and to strip kings of their robes, to open doors before him." Nonetheless, God is Lord alone, and "there is no other" (vv. 5–6). And Israel shall be "saved by the LORD with everlasting salvation" (v. 17). "Turn to me," God says, "and be saved, all the ends of the earth! For I am God, and there is no other" (v. 22). And so, Cyrus's worldly power may be indirectly used by God within His sovereignty to accomplish some preservative ends, but it is not God's way to redeem the world.[16] The difference is of immense importance.

We must acknowledge, then, that it shall be God alone, in His sovereignty, who allows worldly power to be used toward His limited purposes in these cases. And we as Christians cannot choose our ruler to do the work of God in the name of God. And if we dare to give this worldly power the imprimatur of God's redemptive work, our overreaching is sure to incite these powers to go rogue. Horrific abuse is sure to follow. All of this is to say that to assume Trump to be God's Cyrus is to seize hold of worldly power in a way that usurps God and blurs the two powers in the worst of ways. It is a recipe for destruction. It is the premier exemplar of being on the wrong side of power.

This is the issue for all Christians in the aftermath of the January 6 insurrection: How do we resist getting absorbed into worldly power in the name of doing God's work? For to exercise worldly power in the name of God puts us precariously in line to become absorbed into the powers and principalities of evil, the same powers that absorbed those German Christians (*Deutsche Christen*) who with outstretched right arms yelled, "Heil Hitler." Will we swear allegiance to Trump in order to outlaw abortions in the name of God?[17] If we are not to become absorbed into the powers of evil, these are the conversations that every Christian must have and that every church must have in our time.

The Ultimate Lure of Christian Nationalism

There is no more grand illusion of what worldly power can do than the belief in Christian nationalism. Though much contested, the term, simply defined, refers to the belief that a nation's systems of laws, customs, education, and government can be aligned to support a specifically Christian way of life. Most Christians, whether conservative or progressive, Republican or Democrat (in the United States), would agree: our goal should be to impact our culture for Christ's kingdom. Whichever side of issues we are on, the transforming of our culture very much aligns with our belief that the reign of Jesus, His transforming of lives and culture, is a good thing.

The rub comes when we seek to take control of the levers of government to achieve this goal. Using worldly power to force upon people a culture of Christianity in the name of God can only end up in the worst of toxicity, evil, and destruction. Racism, misogyny, and sexual abuse are the result of being filled with the powers gone demonic. And so we must discern the difference between (a) the most modest of preservative goals for justice and (b) the redemptive, transformative goals of justice. The government can achieve the former with legislative enforcement. The latter can be achieved only by the work of the triune God as space opens among peoples, villages, neighborhoods, cities, and countries. We must discern the difference between the two.

To confuse the two goals, asking government to do what only God can do, always works against the work of God among us. Installing "a Christian prince" to "suppress the enemies of God" may sound good, but such coercion does not draw people to God because it is not the way of God.[18] It instead moves people further and further away from God. It ends up with the *Deutsche Christen* supporting Hitler, the Russian Orthodox supporting Putin, evangelicals supporting Trump. The aftermath is a post-Christian culture resistant to God, much like Europe after World War II or Quebec after the "quiet revolution." It sets mission back rather than driving it forward. Christian nationalism is anathema to the mission of God.

Instead, as we enter the world, we are to be salt and light in the world, preserving and illumining, never using the violence of the world to bring more darkness. As we enter our towns and villages and participate in our school boards, local ordinance councils, meeting houses, soup kitchens, and town hall meetings, we must become present, working for good laws, never usurping God. Our goal is never to Christianize the culture, the school systems, or the city hall; it is to make spaces for God to do His work of transforming our towns, our schools, our city hall, and indeed the whole world.

The Ring and the Wrong Side of Power

J. R. R. Tolkien's famed *Lord of the Rings* teaches us that "worldly power" takes its toll on all mortals who dare try to control it. Though there were other rings of power that the evil Sauron used to entice leaders into his orbit of evil, Sauron's ultimate Ring of Power, the One Ring, promised absolute power, and it was the ultimate temptation. This ring tested each person who tried to wield its power for what he or she believed were the true purposes of God. Its allure seems overwhelming. But there is no escaping its eventual corruption despite what good you think you'll do. In the famous words of Gandalf, warning Saruman about the ring, "There is only one Lord of the Ring, only one who can bend it to his will, and he does not share power."[19]

In America today, this is the nature of the temptation we face to be on the wrong side of power. Whether we are conservatives or liberals, Republicans or Democrats, fundamentalists or progressives, Christian nationalism is a manifestation of the wrong side of power. In the words of Brian Zahnd, "Just as Middle-earth could not be saved, only enslaved, by the Ring of Power, so Christianity cannot save the world by political power; it can only be corrupted by it."[20]

But for those of us not tempted by Christian nationalism, there are subtler forms of the temptation to blur the powers that run through our practices of church and through the theologies that bear them. To these we now turn.

5

Playing God with Worldly Power

The More Subtle Temptations

So stay here . . . until you have been clothed with power from on high.

Luke 24:49

Christian nationalism is an obscene version of being on the wrong side of power, of using worldly power for the purposes of God in a country. But there are more mundane versions of this same temptation to blur the powers in the name of God. These temptations work their way subtly through our lives. Christians, every day, with the best of intentions, seek to use whatever worldly power they have to foster a more just and equitable world. What could be wrong with that? As long as such power is used within its limits, nothing is wrong with that. But when we attempt to "play God" with that power, abuse is sure to follow. We must be careful, therefore, never to play God with worldly power. We must be careful, when seeking to rehabilitate an abusive leader in the church, not to rehabilitate them in such a way that they return to the same use of worldly power in the name of God's purposes. We need to discern the wrong side of power so that we return to the right side. We need to discern the blurring of the two powers at work, or we will end up perpetuating more of the same abuse.

In the fall of 2013 eight former elders (who had once guided the leadership) of a megachurch, Harvest Bible Chapel (in the west suburbs of Chicago), sent a letter to the remaining leadership of the church. They stated that James MacDonald, its renowned pastor and a national radio preacher, was disqualified to be the pastor of their church. Quoting 2 Timothy 3:1–5, they listed character traits that prohibit him from being a pastor, including "self-promotion . . . love of money . . . domineering and bullying . . . abusive speech . . . outbursts of anger . . . [and] making misleading statements." They added, "We are prepared to bring forth a host of specific examples and witnesses."[1] These elders were seeing worldly power go off the rails. They were seeing it used abusively in the name of God. They were grappling with the blurring of powers. They were deeply uncomfortable with being on the wrong side of power.

A slew of retorts ensued. Several of the then current Harvest elder board accused the ones sending the letter of defiling the church's reputation. Meanwhile MacDonald, confronted with these allegations, apologized and sought to reconcile with those he had abused. But further abuses were revealed. Financial improprieties were exposed. Stunning episodes of bullying, outbursts of anger, and acts of gaslighting toward individuals were reported. And finally, after recordings of MacDonald's own voice were played on a popular radio show talking blatantly of planting child pornography on the computer of an executive at a Christian publication that had published criticism against him, MacDonald was fired.[2]

Throughout the entire sordid episode, the focus was on MacDonald's character. "Was MacDonald disqualified by his character from being a pastor?" the elders asked. Then, in the aftermath of his firing, bigger questions came to the fore. Parishioners and leaders asked how this church, its governing elders, and its culture could tolerate and even enable such a leader to carry on in such a way for so long without doing anything. People had known for years about his disgusting bullying of people, his rageful tirades against employees, and his abuse of funds, but they had allowed it to go on and even covered it up for him. It was blatant abuse of "power over," but no one said a word.

In the same way, Christian media, theologians, and church officials, when assessing the Harvest situation, focused on the same two factors: (a) it was the character of the leader that was the problem, or (b) it was the culture of the church that enabled such abusive leadership that was the problem. In response, the solutions most offered were (a) the "character solution"—understand and diagnose the leader's narcissism sooner, before it gets out of hand, and provide intervention—or (b) the "culture solution"—cultivate a different culture at the church, a culture that is not dependent upon, and indeed is resistant to, narcissistic, abusive leaders.[3] Nowhere do we see the issue of worldly power versus godly power directly addressed. Nowhere was MacDonald's excessive coercive behavior examined as a symptom of using worldly power wrongly in the name of God—that is, of being on the wrong side of worldly power.

Repeatedly the ruling elder leadership, in the face of awful complaints against MacDonald's abuse of power, would be enamored by the good things God was doing under MacDonald's leadership: all the people coming to church on

Sunday morning; all the people being "fed" by God's Word; the increase in money flows, buildings, and facilities; and the growth of MacDonald's radio ministry. These were all signs that God was working among them through Pastor MacDonald. God was behind MacDonald's flagrant use of worldly "power over" people. This power, therefore, should not be challenged. We must protect and enable this power. In this way the pathway to abuse of demonic proportions was opened. It is the spectacle that happens when a megachurch blurs worldly power with God to keep its impressive programs going. The results are almost always toxic.

So addressing the character of the leader or the culture that enables the leader only gets us so far. Abusive leadership might be curtailed, even held in check for a time, but neither one of these solutions gets to the root of the problem. Worldly power, when used in the name of God, will eventually become unhinged. Abuse is sure to follow. These solutions will prove to be cosmetic solutions at best, like putting a bandage over a metastasizing cancer.

For this reason it is worth examining some everyday scripts in American Christian life, ones that play on the "character solution" or the "culture solution" and can lure Christians into blurring the powers.

Using (Worldly) Power for Justice

"Let us use (worldly) power for the work of God's justice." This is a premier temptation of modern Christians who possess worldly power. There is no more urgent task in God's mission than bringing justice to our world. So why would we not wield any and all means possible to work for God's justice in the world? It is the most compelling and seductive of reasonings and can lead, if we are not careful, to the blurring of the two powers.

Andy Crouch's book *Playing God: Redeeming the Gift of Power* puts forth a compelling version of this reasoning. The book's stated goal is to rehabilitate power by arguing against those "naysayers" who see power as an all-encompassing corrupting force. In the process, Crouch does not distinguish between two different powers. For him, there are two ways the one power is used. For Crouch, we get power right not by distinguishing two kinds of power and then posturing ourselves accordingly, but by discerning the right way to use the power we have. If we use our power in a way that honors God, out of relationship with God, ordered toward His purposes, justice can be accomplished. On the other hand, if we use this power unto ourselves, corruption and abuse happen. If we just refuse to use power at all, we are in essence refusing to live into God's gift, being created in His image. It is an enormously compelling description of power and a compelling explanation of how to use power for God's justice in the world. It is a version of what I have called previously the standard account of power.

And yet perhaps Crouch is tempting us to blur the two powers? To "play God" (in his words) with power? Instead of submitting ourselves to God and His power ("under power"), is Crouch tempting us to use worldly power ("power over") on behalf of God? If so, his book sets us up to do the dangerous thing all over again: to use worldly power in the name of God for God's work, blurring the two powers and thereby putting ourselves on the wrong side of power.

Crouch starts the book by comparing power to electricity. Power, like electricity, is "a fundamental feature of life." "All life requires power." So, much like Reinhold Niebuhr, Crouch claims that power is power, is ubiquitous, and cannot be avoided by anyone who wishes to live in the world. Power is part of creation, a gift given to us by God.[4] And we must use this power as persons created in God's image. This is the reality we are given. In presenting reality in this way, like Niebuhr, Crouch makes any distinction between the two powers irrelevant for work in the world. In essence, he flattens the two powers into one and sets into motion the blurring of the two powers.

Like many evangelicals, Crouch looks to Genesis 1 to establish power as the given we are created with.[5] Humans are commanded to "fill the earth," "subdue it," and have dominion over every living thing. Crouch argues that, as ones created in God's image, we must use this power not in "the struggle for mastery and domination" but in "collaboration, cooperation and ultimately love" for the flourishing of the whole earth.[6] As with many evangelicals, for Crouch, the creation narratives of Genesis form the foundation of a theology of power.[7]

Crouch describes the two contrasting ways one can use power as God's "Let there be . . ." in Genesis 1 and Captain Picard's "Make it so" in *Star Trek*.[8] Picard exercises power by commanding those beneath him, telling them what to do. Anyone under Picard's command is to execute his decision and be done with it. God's command in Genesis, however, bequeaths power to others, making room for more power. "Let there be" opens up space for more power to be distributed. And so, the first way of exercising power creates as God does. The human, in the image of God, gives away power and cultivates the flourishing of life among people. The second way exercises power autonomously, independent of God. This power leads to idolatry, narcissism, and abuse.

Crouch complains that evangelicals jump too quickly to Genesis 3. They do not recognize the goodness of power as created in Genesis 1.[9] But is Crouch missing what happened in Genesis 3 with regard to power? The great sin of humanity in the garden was the usurping of God's power, setting loose the sin of "power over" (Gen. 3:16) and a spiral of that power into violence (6:11) that required the exit of humans from the garden itself, the place of God's presence, godly power. Human agency, by usurping God's power, in independence from God, brought forth a different kind of power, a power of violence to the world, a violence that God renounced (6:6–7). This "power over" must not now somehow be used on the basis of relation to God. It must be either rejected in toto or used as a compromised power in limited fashion in a fallen world. It cannot be used as an extension of God's power to heal the world. This is what leads to abuse. It is why God "drove out the humans" from the garden and placed cherubim and a sword flaming at the entry "to guard the way to the tree of life" (3:24).

To overlook Genesis 3, therefore, is to miss how to live after the fall. There is no getting back to good creation before the fall except through Jesus. We now must deal with a fallen power at work in the world that fundamentally alters how we live with power in the world. We must face the constant choice as we live in the world: whether to live in control of fallen and limited "power over" or to come "under" God's incredible, life-giving "power with" and cooperate with God.

In a small chapter on Jesus, Crouch says, "Jesus knows that, far from being powerless, he holds all things in his hands." In commenting on John 13, where Peter protests Jesus's washing his feet, Crouch curiously says that "Jesus wins." Jesus overcomes resistance and secures obedience from Peter. But even though these things happen, Crouch does not recognize that the power Jesus exercises is a power of another kind. There is no coercion in this power. There is no "power over" in the power of God the Father, through the Son, by the Spirit.

In the entirety of this episode with Peter, Crouch says there is no point "where Jesus gives up power—instead, it is the culmination and demonstration of his power. What Jesus gives up in this story is not power but privilege and status." According to Crouch, Jesus uses His power without apology to heal, forgive, proclaim, teach, and feed thousands, and yet He refuses to use the privilege that comes with those successes.[10] But Crouch fails to see that there is a completely different power at work in and through Jesus. It is indeed a renouncing of worldly power in toto. Crouch sees this as Jesus using the one power in a different way. Power is power, and it is all the same for Crouch. It is just used differently by people who are in right relationship with God. And Jesus is the exemplar in this.

I contend, however, that this account of power blurs the two powers into one. It tempts us to believe that Christians, in right relation to God, can take up worldly power as their own to fulfill God's purposes. It is what leads to abuse in the church and Trumpian Christian politics in the world.

Institutions are good, according to Crouch, when they create and distribute power. They make possible the wherewithal to create something good of the world. They make image-bearing possible.[11] Crouch admits there is an unequal nature to power ("power over") that is exercised in institutions; yet it is for the good, the flourishing of people. He acknowledges this power can devolve into idolatry and injustice. So it must be up to individuals, acting as true image bearers of God, to use the power of an institution toward human flourishing or idolatry and injustice.[12]

And so for Crouch, it is important to get the right people in the positions of power: Christians who are in right relation to God. These are people who will exercise power as image bearers of God, doing the most good for God's justice in the world. We need more Christians to exercise power out of a true relation to God.

And this is where the rubber meets the road, where the ultimate temptation is revealed. It is at this point that Christians are tempted to believe they know best how to run the world. Because of their unique relation to God, they can wield worldly power the best for His purposes. This is the gateway drug to the blurring of the two powers and to the abuse that most often follows. For Crouch, this is the right side of power: Christians in right relation with God in control of power. But, in fact, this is what the wrong side of power looks like.

Crouch is aware this power can be distorted and result in violence. Humans regularly get entangled in sin. The solution for Crouch is the "character solution." Like the elders at Harvest Bible Chapel, Crouch believes the toxicity of those in power can be reordered by leaders submitting to the disciplines of a life with Christ that make them oriented to being "more deeply and truly image bearers" of God. Crouch cites disciplines like solitude, silence, and fasting, solitary disciplines that take us away from an audience that tends to pump up one's ego and instead put us purely before God. For Crouch, these are disciplines that "tame power" and keep it within the purview of its rightful relation to God.[13]

But can these disciplines work this way if they are infused with "power over" in the name of God? Will they not themselves become the means to further the leader's goals in using "power over"? If we do not recognize two different powers at work, how can these disciplines shape a leader so that they come "under" God's power?[14]

Jayakumar Christian runs World Vision, India, an organization of thousands of employees. Crouch marvels as he works for justice at a simple desk, with limited use of phone, engaged with multiple relationships, patiently working to uncover truth. He is much loved by all the people around him as he patiently plods away at freeing child slaves from sweat shops and sex trafficking. He works very simply yet goes deep into systems of corruption and evil to unravel their power over people's lives. For Crouch, this is power at its best.

But a closer look at Jayakumar begs the question: Is this a man exercising "power over" or a man who has submitted to "under power," God's power at work in the world? Does the power at work in Jayakumar look like "coercion/power over" or, rather, the power unleashed in Jesus by His death, resurrection, and ascension as Lord of the world? This question eludes Crouch, but it must not elude us. Because it will make all the difference in our churches, the posture of our leaders, and the Christians we send into the world. It will enable us to avoid the blurring of the two powers. It will open space for God to work among us in His power, for us to be on the right side of God's power.

Crouch fails to recognize how radically different the power of God is from the "power over" that dominates the world after the fall. But by proclaiming a new power at work in Jesus, we can challenge the use of "power over" at all times among Christian leadership. We can keep worldly power within its limits when we are in the world. And where we can make space for God's presence to work, we must. For He alone, in His power, can convict of sin, pull us toward His love, draw us toward Him and one another, and work wonderous healing, reconciliation, and renewal of all things relational and systemic.

Keep (Worldly) Power Safe from Abuse (The Culture Solution)

"Let us redeem (worldly) power from abuse." This too is a modern temptation toward blurring the two powers. Found often in churches that have just experienced a failed leader, this temptation entices us to believe that we can rehabilitate (worldly) power for God's kingdom by recognizing its dangers and putting guardrails around it to keep those in power from abusing it. This approach, however, will fail if it does not distinguish between the two powers and engage each one accordingly. If we seek to redeem worldly power for God's redemptive work, we will be tempted all over again to play God, with its attendant abuse waiting in the wings for its next horrific eruption.

Diane Langberg's book *Redeeming Power: Understanding Authority and Abuse in the Church* lays out a compelling case for redeeming power from abuse. As a therapist and authority on trauma and abuse, she offers multiple interventions, ways of noticing red flags in leaders and confronting systems that enable abusive leaders. She instructs churches on how to shape the character of leaders toward Christ and Christlike ways of using power, thereby avoiding abuse. It is a sobering and yet hopeful presentation of a way forward for churches in the midst of abusive leadership and toxic cultures.

And yet this very process could be the means by which we are tempted into thinking we can be the ones who, by virtue of our relationship to Christ, can use (worldly) power in a way that is safe from abuse. Langberg makes us aware of the abusive dangers of this power. She urges us to be vigilant against the abuse of such power. But Langberg, like Crouch, does not describe an alternative power at work in Christ that requires an entirely different human relation to power. And so Christians are tempted to use power in a way that is susceptible to the hubris and dangers of exercising worldly power on behalf of God.

Langberg states, as her opening thesis, that "power is inherent in being human. Even the most vulnerable among us have power. How we use it or withhold it determines our impact on others."[15] She defines "power" as "having the capacity to do something, to act or produce an effect, to influence people or events, or to have authority." "By our sheer presence in this world, we, God's image bearers, have power."[16] And so Langberg, like Crouch, and like Niebuhr, flattens out power into one power, worldly "power over." There is no distinction between two powers. Power is ubiquitous, and we cannot live without it, so we must choose how to use it.

Like Crouch, Langberg turns to the Genesis creation story to frame the nature of power. She says, "God made humans who bear his likeness and told them to rule." Man and woman together "are to take the power God granted them and use it for good." But they succumbed to the temptation to be like God, and so they "used their power to choose evil when the power ought to have borne the likeness of God and been used to choose good."[17] And so, as for Crouch, for Langberg, power is power and is given from God, and the problem with power is that it is used wrongfully, for evil purposes. She does not recognize that God's power and His very agency were usurped by humans in the fall. Langberg doesn't recognize that the very power itself is the problem and that our relationship to worldly power must change so that we can submit to and participate in God's power.

At one point in the book Langberg seems to grant a nod to this dynamic. She uses several stories of persons using power in good ways. In the middle of this section, she describes how "godly power is derivative, it comes from a source outside us. It is always used under God's authority . . . exercised in humility . . . as his servants . . . for the end goal of bringing glory to God."[18] Wonderfully, Langberg describes submission to God as the posture necessary in order for us to come "under" God's power. Langberg comes so close to recognizing a different power, a different source of that power, and a different posture necessary to participate in that power. She comes close to everything described in this book as the right side of power.

Nonetheless, the whole construct of exercising power "over" others never gets dislodged. In the ensuing stories that illustrate her understanding of power, there may be hints of how God is at work through His power, but ultimately it is human persons in charge exercising the power. The Brazilian pastor living among the alcoholics, the Arab woman speaking truth to power, the gracious sheikh are all illustrations of how "God would have *us* exercise our power," in her words.[19] Power is our power, to be used in certain ways, and we remain the ones in control of it.

Langberg asks how so much abuse happens in the church at the hands of leaders. She says it starts with self-deception. "We are too generous in our self-trust."[20] She shows how even Hitler used Christian ideals to deceive himself and a people. Her solution? "If we follow [Christ], then whatever we do as individuals in our families, our churches, our communities, or this world that does not look like Christ, we will both repent of and abandon."[21] We just need integrity, so that "words and flesh are . . . one."[22] Jesus is our example. Follow Him.

But we must ask Langberg how so many claiming to sincerely follow Christ fall into the snares of using worldly power abusively, all in the name of following Jesus. Their own self-deception gets them. It is the failure to distinguish between the two powers that is the culprit. Without distinguishing between the two powers, we are ever tempted to take control of worldly power and use it in God's unchallengeable name. It is, I contend, the recipe for abuse.

Langberg describes how "worldly" power (without describing it this way) works in toxic systems. There is hierarchy in it: "power over." She describes how "close followers" of powerful leaders protect their leaders and the "positions and the power that goes with them" that they hold in these systems. It all works together in a toxic cocktail. Then the followers of these leaders take on the identity of being part of the "we" who commit allegiance to the one with "power over" at all costs because their very life/meaning is at stake. So the whole system gets ordained by God. Langberg incisively describes how the whole system develops to protect the (worldly) power that abuses people.[23]

Langberg seems to believe we will solve this power's problems by recognizing it, calling it out, and keeping these toxic effects in check (the "culture solution"). In so doing we can create a culture that is able to order power toward goodness. All the while, however, the problem of "power over" never gets called out. "Power over" still operates, simmering within the system.

Langberg proposes, like Crouch, that the shaping of the character of the leader is paramount to the problem of power. She makes the rather stunning statement that "the Atlantic slave trade, segregation in US schools, and the Nazi regime were all powerful systems that were changed by one person—William Wilberforce, Martin Luther King Jr., Dietrich Bonhoeffer—influencing others."[24] We might be tempted by Langberg to think that I, as a single individual, can make a difference with my power if I will but take care to shape my character before God. We might be tempted to believe it is up to me to take hold of worldly power and use it to change the world.

But another story is at work behind Langberg's heroes (which I'll outline in the epilogue of this book). An amazing on-the-ground abolitionist movement stood behind Wilberforce and behind Student Nonviolent Coordinating Committee prayer meetings of White and Black persons together taking place throughout the Jim Crow South that gave birth to Martin Luther King Jr.; and indeed, Bonhoeffer died in a concentration camp, and his life impacted the world only after he had been martyred. These networks, interrelational grids of people groups, and martyrdom were all signs of a different power at work than worldly power.

There is so much good in Langberg's work. Her dissection of character and how it gets toxified by power and then supported by a culture that itself turns toxic is a must-read for all who lead and work in churches. Her discussions of "sitting with trauma," listening, grieving, lamenting, describe so well the basics of making space for godly power to work among us to heal, redeem, restore.[25] She describes compellingly the ways in which Jesus's use of power is starkly different from worldly power. A bit like Crouch, she calls for a different way of exercising power: the way of Jesus. But, unfortunately, the "power over" is kept in place.[26] And so I fear that until we distinguish the two powers, we remain under the allure of worldly power, believing we can be the ones to play God with worldly power and redeem worldly power for God. It is, I fear, a sure recipe for the abuse Langberg works so hard to rid us of.

Leverage Your Privilege

"Let us leverage our privilege for justice in a broken, unjust world." This too can be a temptation to blur the powers, perhaps the subtlest one yet. This call, stated well by Dominique Gilliard in his book *Subversive Witness*, states that "God calls privileged people to strategically leverage access, influence, and resources to subvert the status quo and advance the kingdom."[27] This call is compelling. But does it lead us into yet another way to blur the powers, use worldly power in the name of God, and be on the wrong side of power? Do we thus perpetuate the abuse of privilege on even more persons?

Privilege is power that enables people to accomplish things, access money, and possess opportunity inequitably, giving them advantages over those who do not have privilege. It comes in many forms, including race, gender, citizenship, class, education, and sexual orientation. Gilliard says privilege is "stackable," so that some persons possess multiple privileges of status, class, race, gender, and citizenship all because of who they are, where they come from, or to whom they were born.[28] And so privilege is "power over" inherited from "within" systems that privileged people exert, sometimes unknowingly, within and by the systems, to influence circumstances and people to the advantage of the one with the privilege.

The first step for Gilliard is for those with privilege to become aware of that privilege. We can't leverage privilege if we continue to deny its existence.[29] The discipline of locating our privilege enables all who have it to see this power at work subliminally in their cultures. It illumines the subtle forms of coercion, violence, and exclusion exercised by the majority that go unchecked in the culture. The "privilege" discourse helps people expose the injustices woven deep into the systems of one's culture.

And so "leverage your privilege" narrates persuasively how we can use this power subversively (against the system) toward the undoing of racism and other forms of injustice, to reshape a culture. Gilliard's proposal is another take on the "culture solution." Let us use our privilege in the culture to subvert the system (or the culture) built on the privilege. In other words, let us use "power over" to undermine the negative effects of "power over."

The question of this chapter, however, asks of Gilliard: Is there an avenue here to blur the two powers in the worst of ways when we use privilege to subvert privilege? When we use privilege as a form of "power over," in the name of God's kingdom, do we end up perpetuating that same privilege, exposing people to the same inequities, abuses, and exclusions that privilege always brings with it—only this time endorsed by God?

As we've already seen (with both Crouch and Langberg), the first step in blurring the two powers is to make "power over" the only power. The power of God in Jesus is secluded away to work in our souls only. We then essentialize "power over," saying that it is everywhere, inescapable and inevitable. Our only choice, therefore, is to use it (for God's purposes) or lose it. Is Gilliard leaning this direction when he says, "It is undeniable that God entrusts people with privilege and power, with a missional purpose of creating life, flourishing, and fostering shalom where death, destruction and oppression have reigned for far too long"?[30]

Gilliard does not shy away from the problems of privilege. He says, "Racism, patriarchy, classism, and other forms of privilege—and the isms that produce these privileges—are not of God." These privileges and the "disparities that flow from them are the consequences of sin."[31] Gilliard knows there's something deeply wrong about this privilege, yet he believes it still can be used for Christ's kingdom. How do we use such privilege as Christians?

As already alluded to, Gilliard calls us to leverage privilege itself to subvert the existing structures of privilege. For Gilliard, there are ways we can use privilege to make space for repentance, to stand in solidarity with the unprivileged, and otherwise disrupt the systems of privilege themselves. This is what I believe Gilliard argues for.[32]

But could it be this easy?

Think of me, an older White male, occupying influence because of my ethnicity, my learning of the ways of power, my education, my access to money, influence, and decision-making power. I am looked up to and reverenced because of what? The way I operate? My degrees? My posturing? My inherited pedigree? The way the culture has trained people to defer to me? What does it mean for me to use this privilege or to pass on the advantages of this privilege to others who don't have it? Is it a good thing that I pass on this form of worldly power that is based in these learned cultural postures, hierarchies, and presumptions that cause people to defer to me?

Furthermore, am I the one, formed and jaded by this privilege, who should shepherd that privilege toward the underprivileged? Should I be the one to influence who should be the ones chosen to be platformed? Will this not perpetuate these same diseased ways of power? And yet, if I am to use my privilege, I must be the one behind its use to help others benefit from it. Am I to be the one to use "power over" to direct the "power over" to others who can use it for righteous ends? Add on to this the question, When I associate Christ's name with this privileging, have I not baptized this kind of privilege with a veneer of righteousness and unleashed it in even more hideous and unchecked ways?

Feminist anti-racism scholar Peggy McIntosh, in her groundbreaking essay on privilege in the 1980s, wrote that "privilege" carries "the connotation of being something everyone must want." But then she describes what privilege does, how it "confers dominance, gives permission to control because of one's race or sex." She says this privilege "gives license to some people to be, at best, thoughtless, and at worst, murderous." She says it distorts the way we see people. Unless it is rejected, McIntosh argues, it will "always reinforce our present hierarchies," the systems that oppress and destroy people's lives.[33]

And so, as with all forms of "power over," we must be cautious about the use of privilege. Yes, it can be used to accomplish some preservative measures of justice, manage some equality among persons, allow others to participate in the existing power structures, and provide some inclusion and opportunity within the system. But can it truly subvert the systems of injustice it perpetuates? Or will we who have privilege be tempted to exercise our privilege in the name of God unhinged from God, so that now its posturing and diminishment of persons are sure to follow?

And once using privilege, are we limiting what can be accomplished for justice? Is a world possible without privilege? Could not God's power through His presence make space for healing, reconciliation, and an entirely new way to live and be together in the tasks of our daily lives, a way of life in which privilege no longer exists?

To illustrate the subversive leveraging of privilege, Gilliard expounds on one of Jesus's encounters: His meeting with the chief tax collector Zacchaeus, narrated in Luke 19:1–10.[34] He describes in depth the Roman system of tax collection that Zacchaeus was a part of. Jesus, Gilliard says, calls Zacchaeus to repentance. Jesus declares that salvation has come to Zacchaeus's house after Zacchaeus gives half of his possessions to the poor. In terms of the money he has stolen, Zacchaeus will make things right by paying it back four times (v. 8). For Gilliard, Jesus uses His privilege to influence Zacchaeus toward his repentance and these reparations.

But did Jesus use any cultural privilege in regard to Zacchaeus or the system? He went to Zacchaeus's house, "stayed" with him, ate with him, and became his "guest." These are actions of someone who has gone "among" the persons involved, not "over," someone who assumes no privilege. Sitting at a table was an act of fellowship, becoming an equal among others as family, giving up any postures of privilege, especially if one goes as a "guest" (v. 7). What Jesus did was an affront to those around Him, because He did not posture Himself over against the hated tax collector. It was out of this space of nonprivilege that Zacchaeus was transformed, that he was saved, and indeed his whole house became a manifestation of that salvation.

Zacchaeus could have made things right according to the system and its encoded privileges. But instead of using the system, he called Jesus "Lord" and entered into a new system of God's kingdom. He gave up half his wealth (he did not hold on to it to leverage it). The normal recompense for money stolen within the system, by fraud, was to repay it in full plus a tenth. Zacchaeus went beyond anything required of him within the system of privilege.[35] It appears, then, that Jesus does not use or leverage privilege or ask Zacchaeus to do the same. Jesus offers an alternative beyond leveraging your privilege. It is by the pure power of His presence at a table that disruption and subversion happen. And the result is an overthrow of the system, as opposed to a using of it.

Jesus did not ask the rich young ruler to use his immense privilege; He told him, "Go, sell what you own, and give the money to the poor, and you will have treasure in heaven; then come, follow me" (Mark 10:21). In Philippians 2, a passage I've dwelled on previously in this book, the apostle makes it clear that Jesus did not regard His divine status as "something to be exploited" (v. 6). Rather, He "emptied himself" of the privilege. He entered the world to be among people, where He made space for the power of God to be unleashed wherever He was physically present.

God may have used the privilege of Joseph ruling over Egypt to preserve the people of Israel from starvation through a seven-year famine.[36] Through the entire Bible, we see God allowing things to get done by persons in worldly power that help people survive, be preserved for another day, prevent horrific violence, prevent overt injustice, and perform other preservative functions. These are indirect uses of worldly power that are allowed to work preservative acts within God's sovereignty. But they come with a cost. They never accomplish the redemptive healing work of God's justice. The power used by Joseph enslaved God's people (Gen. 47:19, 25). And so eventually it was God's power that would have to work to liberate Israel and allow them to flourish amid the unjust systems perpetuated by Joseph.[37]

And so let us acknowledge that it is a net good to recognize where privilege is used abusively and with blindness. Let us acknowledge that we can sometimes use our privilege to subvert systems, mitigate abuses, and improve people's situations in life amid injustice. But let us also be careful to recognize the limits of what privilege can accomplish: minimal, preservative measures of justice. Ultimately, the abuse in a social system cannot be subverted while we use the very source of that abuse to do so. Let us be mindful that it is only on the right side of God's power where true transformative healing disrupts a system and brings restorative change to the social systems in which we live.

Character or Culture or Another Power?

Oxford political theorist Brian Klaas, in his 2021 book *Corruptible: Who Gets Power and How It Changes Us*, argues that "too much attention is paid to the notion that power corrupts. Not enough attention is paid to why corruptible people seek power."[38] Drawing on numerous sociological studies, Klaas says that it is the culture of power as presented by the organization that attracts narcissistic persons already addicted to coercive power to their positions of leadership.[39] Klaas favors the "culture solution" (that it is the culture that attracts abusive leaders) in combination with the "character solution" (we can avoid the bad characters by changing the culture) for preventing the abusive leader from gaining power.

But we have seen how the problem of power is so much more than this for the Christian. For the church of Jesus Christ, it is imperative that we eschew both the one who leads with worldly power and a position of leadership that projects the use of worldly power. The choice between character and culture goes away. All leaders must lead in humility, a posture of "under" God's power. And the culture of a place where people follow Jesus should ooze with this kind of practice. This is what it means for the church to be the people of Jesus, who are "under" His power.

To be clear, Crouch, Langberg, and Gilliard all offer ways to control (worldly) power for justice and keep it from going off the rails and thus wreaking havoc and abuse in people's lives. And so we should be grateful for their work. They offer ways to make use of worldly power and keep it within guardrails when this is the only power we have to use. But the temptations to live on the wrong side of power and take up worldly power in the name of God for His purposes remain; the disease of worldly power continues to simmer beneath. The eruption of abuse lies ever close because worldly power corrupts the individual and toxifies the cultural systems whenever it is used in the name of God and for His purposes.

The episode of James MacDonald teaches us that the only way to healing, the only way to transforming culture, is to become communities that persistently refuse to live on the wrong side of power. Let us regularly practice distinguishing the two powers and resisting all urges to put worldly power to use under the name and purposes of God's redemptive work. This is the diagnosis we need in order to avoid the next Harvest Bible Chapel incident. This is the practice we need in order to make space for that other kind of power, the power of the living God, to inhabit our lives, our churches, and our way of life in the world.

You're Doing It Again

One summer night, there was an incident between police and a group of Hispanic persons in our town. A man who was in the group, a friend of mine, told me the whole story. A Hispanic family was ticketed five hundred dollars for having a car parked over the public sidewalk at the end of their driveway. Mexican immigrants in our town often lived in a housing unit with two or three families. Some members of the families worked two jobs. As a result, there were more cars in the family than could be parked in any given driveway. The public ordinance ticketing cars perched over a sidewalk was especially harmful to these families. I decided to call a meeting. I would exert my ministerial and White male authority in a community, an authority that the police would no doubt respect.

But one of my fellow ministers warned me. She said, "Dave, you're doing it again. Your privilege is showing." If I called this meeting, she advised, and held it in our church building, on my terms, that would set the terms for all future meetings. I protested. I would surely make space for all voices. But my privilege, by my mere presence and my words, would still set the terms. Any achievements would be made based on that privilege. And indeed, any future disputes probably would center me, the older White male leader, as the moderator. I would be the first one Hispanic persons would go to to enforce the terms. Any accommodations made by police and ordinance committees would be seen as under my purview.

Some good no doubt would still be accomplished if I took charge and used my worldly power. There would be an opportunity to address the ordinance and change it for parking multiple vehicles in a driveway space. Some preservative justice might come out of this. But would a new understanding between police, Hispanic immigrants in our town, and the rest of the populations take place? Would a mutuality of forgiveness, understanding, and connection happen that would reframe how police and those of Mexican descent engaged one another in our village? Would a transformed village happen? There was room for so much more.

My ministerial comrade suggested that our Hispanic brothers and sisters call the meeting, hold it in a place they felt was home, and lead the conversation. Let us give up "power over" and seek to submit ourselves to the God of Jesus Christ, who is at work among us. Let us pray for God's Spirit to work and then give witness to Jesus, who is healing the world. Immediately it hit me, how much this kind of thinking takes an imagination for another kind of power at work in our lives.

Making Space for the Power of the Spirit

This is the challenge that lies before us amid the rubble of today's church, which has succumbed to worldly power. Will we as Christians, as pastors, as churches continue to operate out of worldly power, enforcing character solutions or culture solutions in the hopes of achieving minimal outcomes that feed our egos? Or will we make space for the Holy Spirit, the power of the risen Christ unleashed wherever He rules, wherever the Holy Spirit is made space for?

The day after the resurrection, the new world had begun, a new power had been unleashed. The victory over all the powers of the world had been won, and we find the disciples in the upper room. The doors are locked. They are frightened, protecting themselves, unaware of what has happened. Their ways of worldly power have been dashed, and Jesus enters the room.

He stands among them and says, "Peace be with you" (John 20:19). It is a statement of the awesome power and the presence of Jesus. He shows them His body, His scars, and somehow they see that He is the Lord, and He says to them again, "Peace be with you" (v. 21). The presence of the Lord, His peace bringing power, shall be the foundation upon which their lives shall proceed. And then He sends them out of that room into the world by breathing on them, saying, "Receive the Holy Spirit" (v. 22).

The Holy Spirit must be received. She cannot be controlled. This is the power upon which they will live with open hands in submission to Jesus, under His power. This is not worldly power. This is the very keys of the kingdom (Matt. 16:19). This is real, earthshaking, life-changing power that they shall live under and cooperate with. "If you forgive the sins of any, they are forgiven them; if you retain the sins of any, they are retained" (John 20:23). But it is a different power than the world knows. This is the power unleashed in the death and resurrection of Jesus.

Before Christ ascends, He sends them again into the world. He tells them, "Stay here in the city until you have been clothed with power from on high" (Luke 24:49). They are being sent under a different power. They must not move forward under any other power. This is who they are. This is who we are. This is how God will change the world.

There are many forms of "power over," some more congenial to our Christian tastes than others. There are ways to justify the use of worldly power with the highest intentions. But God is calling the church to more. As we saw earlier, if Jesus is not at the center of our lives and the ways we lead and move in the world, we will end up leading with "power over." And all our work shall either be limited to minimalist achievements (preservative in nature) or end up in narcissism, abuse, and destruction. Without Jesus at the center, without making space for the Spirit to work, without coming under Her power, we will end up taking over control all over again. In the words of that pastor to me, we'll end up doing it all over again.

But our calling is to become a people who place Jesus at the center and make space for the Spirit to work; to become such a church is our mantle. But where do we start? How would we be different? We turn now to ponder what being such a people in the world might look like. What will be the practices that shape our lives into and under Christ's power among us?

6

Living under the Power of Christ

The Church on the Right Side of Power

> Submit yourselves one to another out of reverence to Christ.
>
> Ephesians 5:21 (AT)

A New Imagination

Several years ago, while speaking at a gathering of pastors and Christian leaders, I presented for two days on how God through Jesus desires to work in our churches/organizations. The main thrust of the presentation was that leaders must make space for God's power to work in our churches. We must give up the techniques of worldly power, the techniques we have become so dependent upon to get things done. These techniques, and their money, help organize big events, social justice projects, and massive children's/teen's programs.

These techniques often accomplish immediate, visible results. We might even see increased attendance, improved budgets, or some social justice projects hit the headlines of our local news outlets. And yet, despite these successes, the evidence is that we are not impacting our world for Christ. We are turning Christians into consumers of a thin Christianity. And even though several churches might grow big by doing these things, Christianity as a whole is dying a slow death in our country, a country that is being secularized more by the day.

Worst of all, in relying on worldly power, our churches have crowded out the living Christ, in all of His power, from doing His saving, transformative work among us. We have lost who we are as a people of God's revolutionary power to bring healing, reconciliation, and transformation into the towns and villages where we live. We have blended into irrelevancy.

I challenged the leaders to turn away from the production of church, the measuring of success by the size of buildings, crowds, or budgets. Through Jesus, let us give up the control techniques, submit to His reign, from whence the Holy Spirit shall rush in, convict, speak, bring people together, forgive, reconcile, heal, activate, energize, and inhabit the work of Christ's people. Let us gather people into our worship gatherings, but also into our homes and among the poor, where people can be present to each other and the power and presence of the risen Christ can be released among us.

As I led our final session for the conference, I asked the pastors and leaders, "Is this possible?" I asked them to write down on a piece of paper every reason they thought this would not be possible when they returned to their places of ministry. Then we gathered up the pieces of paper and assembled a list of the "top ten reasons for why this will never work at your church (or organization)." As I sat before them on a raised chair, we started to read the list and debrief. The pastor/leaders said things like the following: "If my congregation doesn't see x, y, and z, they will stop coming and the budget will implode." "My people will say I'm not leading the church and ask me to resign." "People expect a strong leader." "People will say, 'But we've always done it this way.'" "We'll never get anything done if we do it this way." "I am evaluated by my board every year as to how effective my leadership is. They would have no idea how to assess my leadership. This would end my employment."

The "top ten reasons" list illustrates the profound lack of imagination in the Western church for how God might work apart from worldly power. Worldly power is woven into the cultures of American church. Our churches are addicted to worldly power as the means for Christians to get things done. In the various places of leadership in the church, classroom, business, and boards of Christian and secular organizations, we strive for the influence and the immediate advantages that worldly power brings. And yet history confirms: God works and overcomes the same-old-same-old to do marvelous things through those who can give up worldly power to make space for the risen Lord, in the power of the Holy Spirit, to be among us and work for His purposes. But we have no imagination.

There is no how-to manual for discerning worldly power from God's power. Certainly there are red flags that indicate worldly power is already at work, as already discussed. But to shape a culture into God's power, we need practices that over time cultivate a different-from-the-world way of being in relation to God's power. Such practices will make space for godly power and, in the process, subvert worldly power. They will gradually shape a culture to be on the right side of power, leading us toward openness and submission to God's power at work among us. Often, these practices will be rejected by those caught in the habits of worldly power. But, to quote an old song, "It only takes a spark to get a fire going." The smallest opening for God to work can lead to bigger changes. Years down the road the slow ferment of righteousness, goodness, and justice infects not only our churches but our neighborhoods, our towns, and even our country. Our cultures are transformed. And people are welcomed into the kingdom.

Here are just a few such practices and situations where they might be applied.

Mutual Submission

Mutual submission is the practice of two or more persons submitting to the presence of God and to each another to make a decision, negotiate a conflict or disagreement, or find a way forward in a situation. Mutual submission subverts worldly "power over" and the antagonism of "who wins," and it makes space for God's power to work among us.[1]

In Ephesians 5:21, the apostle Paul writes, "Be subject to one another out of reverence for Christ." It is the framing sentence for all that is to follow, what has become known as the household code (*Haustafel*) in Ephesians. In this one text, Paul prescribes how to live in all social relations, including the marital relationship, family relationships, and the economic relationships of the day. With each case, Paul upends the "power over" of his present day and turns the relation into a mutuality between people who come under the power and presence of Jesus the Lord. It is in this practice of mutual submission that the hold of "power over" is broken and the power of His inbreaking reign through the Holy Spirit is invited in. The practice of mutual submission, when done well, can take us from the wrong side of power to the right side.

The text reads, "Be subject to one another out of reverence for Christ" (Eph. 5:21). The action of "submitting yourselves" (KJV) depends on the prior injunction (vv. 18–20) to be filled with the Spirit, singing songs to the Lord and giving thanks. It is the bringing of oneself under ("out of reverence") the revered reign of the anointed Messiah. Paul's word "reverence" speaks to a fear and trembling that come before the very real presence of God at work in our midst.[2]

There can be no submitting to one another if we do not trust that a power of a different kind from worldly power is at work in this space. We must truly trust that there is another power at work here—God's power—in order to give up control and let God work. Both persons must be equally submitted to one another. And in this space, a new metaphysic of power makes possible the transformation of our lives and the places where we worship, live, and work.

The word "submit" is a much-despised word in current-day church and secular cultures.[3] Its presence in Ephesians 5:22 has been used by men to abuse wives and women in general in hideous ways. The word itself has justified the use of abusive power over people in the name of God and the authority of Scripture. But once we notice how the apostle Paul uses the word, we gain insight into how the practice of submission, rightly inhabited, breaks the hold of worldly "power over" and makes space for the power of God to work in a social space, a relationship, an organization.

In Ephesians 5:22–33, the apostle redescribes marriage, family, and economy so that the relations between wife and husband, child and parent, slave and master are no longer one over the other, but mutual self-giving. It could be missed, but in contrast to the patriarchy and hierarchies of the day, the redescription is stunning in its mutuality. It is the presence and reign of another power at work between the parties that make such mutuality possible. Christ is present throughout the description of marriage (vv. 23, 24, 25, 29, 32). In Ephesians 6, the children's relation to the parents is "in the Lord" (v. 1), and the fathers raise their children never toward anger but also "in the discipline and instruction of the Lord" (v. 4). And slaves obey their masters as they obey Christ, as slaves of Christ, as serving the Lord, not human beings (vv. 5–8). The passage on slaves and masters is an entire redescription of the slave's relationship to their master. And then Paul says, "Masters, do the same." There can be no threatening of the slave by the master, for they both have the same master in heaven (v. 9). Allowing that the Greco-Roman form of economic slavery was vastly culturally different from the chattel slavery of the Euro-colonialist United States, it is a stunning redescription of all and any economic relations.

Mutual submission, then, is the practice of giving up of worldly power over another by both parties, showing patience, and making space for the careful tending to the presence of God in Christ among the two parties.

But who goes first? It is assumed that because the wife, the child, and the slave go first in each relational submission, they are the ones devoid of power. But the Greek word for "submit" in Ephesians 5:21 (and applied to all that follows) is the same as in Romans 13:1, where Paul is asking the Christians to be subject to a foreign (and persecuting) government. Just as Paul is not asking the Christians to submit to everything the Roman government asks, including martyrdom at the hand of the state, so Paul here is not asking the wife to submit to her abusive husband or agree with everything he puts forth. The act of submission in this context should actually be seen as a position of strength and conviction. Out of this strength the woman challenges the husband or the foreign government to seek the Lord, who is at work. The one who goes first is the strong one.

We see this in church leadership, when a circle of leaders is gathered to discern the way forward on an issue in the church. In prayer, we trust God is at work among us. And then the one who has brought an important issue to the team or has a conviction as to what should be done puts forth a proposal. They say, "I propose A" in an act of leadership. And then they will say to the group, "I submit to you" (an act of strength, not weakness). A conversation ensues. Proposal A is seen from multiple viewpoints. The one gifted in faith or pastoral concerns speaks from their gift. And the proposal is changed and adjusted until we as a group can say together, "We have the mind of Christ" (1 Cor. 2:16).

All the gifts shall be manifest in a group making decisions like this. Most often the one gifted as apostle will be the one making a proposal, pushing the conversation forward, summarizing and asking, "Do we have a consensus?" The pastors, teachers, evangelists, and prophets in the room, and those possessing any other gifts, must be given space to speak. The apostle and those with all the other gifts must be respected. There will be leadership in the group, often given by the apostle, but it will be leadership born out of mutuality.[4]

In moments of deadlock, when worldly power seems to have its grip on a relationship, and it is you versus me, it is the one in perceived power who must go first in submitting. Whether in marriage or in a megachurch, between a pastor and another leader, if there is a sniff of worldly power at work, the person perceived to have worldly power must go first and submit to the other(s). In this way, worldly power is broken. It is almost inevitable that space then opens for the others to submit as well. And God can speak, convict, and work.

This is most visibly modeled by Jesus at the table in Luke 22. Jesus has already taken His "place at the table" (v. 14). The disciples are jockeying for position in the coming kingdom

(v. 24). They are heatedly arguing for positions of worldly "power over," and Jesus shuts it down, saying that it shall be "not so among you" (v. 26). He explains, "I confer on you, just as my Father has conferred on me, a kingdom" (v. 29). He is pointing to the table and new relationships made possible in mutuality under godly power. It is here, most likely, that Jesus illustrates the giving up of worldly power by washing the disciples' feet. Peter protests (John 13:8). He cannot imagine another way of power. But Jesus says, "Unless I wash you"—unless Peter accepts this new understanding of power—"you have no share with me." A stunning redescription of the relationship of lordship and power ensues (vv. 15–16). The spell of worldly power is broken. Mutual submission opens space for transformation and for God to work.

Again, having said all of this, we should never assume that the word "submit" is asking the early Christians to put themselves in harm's way. As with the Roman government (which is persecuting Christians) in Romans 13:1, so also a wife should never submit herself to the abuse of her husband, nor a staff worker to an abusive pastor. If there is danger—say, with a staff person going to an abusive pastor—the staff person should take a trusted friend (or two) along to a meeting with a suspected abuser. If the staff person submits a truth to the pastor and the pastor refuses to submit in return, the staff person should flee. This meeting is the revealing that this is not the church of Jesus Christ. It is an organization operating in worldly power in the name of Christ only.

As we have seen countless times, whenever worldly power over is used in the name of Christ, this is the recipe for abuse that takes the form of multiple evils. The staff person should therefore leave, shake the dust off his or her sandals, and declare anathema, that God is not being allowed to work here (Matt. 10:14–15; Acts 13:51–52). Likewise, a wife should leave the abusive husband. Churches should encourage these kinds of safe meetings, wary of the revealing that can happen. The person who submits is not only strong when submitting first but also strong when fleeing as a witness to the reality that God is no longer at work here. These kinds of meetings are revolutionary, tending toward revealing and transforming cultures of churches.

I remember being with a group of elders at a church that was locked in a dispute between three pastors. For over a year this dispute was locked in a tug-of-war of worldly power. Who was more at fault? Who was more to blame than the other? Who was going to win? The dispute was locked into the frame of worldly power. As I sat there listening to this group of twelve elders (not all of them men), the conversation pointed to George as being the one who was manipulative in his leadership. George was the one in power in worldly power terms. I counseled George that it was up to him to confess first and submit to what he could honestly own as his sin, his participation in injustice. He refused. The other two pastors, he said, were more at fault. I agreed with him. But I said that by going first, he would break the logjam of "power over," allowing room for the power of the Spirit to work. He eventually did go first, confessing his sin in front of the entire church. In the weeks that followed, the other pastors repented and revealed much more heinous acts of manipulation and injustice. One left. But over time, George was wonderfully forgiven and welcomed into full fellowship by the congregation. Congregation members were wonderfully healed and strengthened, and trust was rebuilt. The hold of worldly "power over" the congregation had been broken because the one in perceived power submitted first. The space of mutuality was opened up for the Holy Spirit to do Her work.

The practice of mutual submission pulls the rug out from under worldly power and transforms what's left into a relational space for God to manifest His power in Jesus Christ. It is a space of surrender, self-abandonment, and calmness unlike anything the world knows.[5] It lies at the core of all the church's main practices. It is what makes space for the power of the Holy Spirit to work among us. Mutual submission is a sign that the church is living on the right side of power.

The Plurality of Gifts

The practice of the plurality of gifts gathers the leadership into a circle of leaders who listen to all voices and receive all the gifts, with Jesus at the center from which God can work to lead a people. Such a practice in leadership shapes the whole church to gather in mutuality of the gifts under the power of Christ in discipleship and mission. Practicing the plurality of the gifts subverts worldly power and makes space for God's power to work among us, causing a community to grow into what the apostle Paul refers to as "the fullness of Christ" (Eph. 4:13 NASB), the fullness of the power and presence of the living Christ.

In 1 Corinthians 12, the apostle describes the functioning of the body of Christ through the gifts. "There are varieties of gifts, but the same Spirit," "varieties of services, but the same Lord," and "varieties of activities, but it is the same God who activates all of them in everyone" (vv. 4–6). We are therefore to mutually depend upon one another's gifts. No one person is to inhabit all the gifts. And "the eye cannot say to the hand, 'I have no need of you'" (v. 21). The weaker is just as indispensable as the strong (v. 22). It could not be any clearer. We are to rely upon one another's giftings mutually. No one gift is above another.

This is the way godly power is unleashed: the gifts. In Ephesians 4 it is the Lord, who has ascended to all authority

(vv. 7–9), who then gives "the gifts" and fills the body through these gifts with His power so as to grow us to "the fullness of Christ" (NASB), the fullness of the power of His presence (v. 13). Likewise, in Romans 12, the apostle teaches that "we have gifts that differ according to the grace given to us" (v. 6). Each of us is given these gifts "according to the measure of faith that God has assigned" (v. 3). So all are to exercise these gifts within the limits given to each one, in submission to His presence among us, individually as "members of one another" (v. 5).

In each of these passages, the Christian is to enter the social space of God's people with humility, in submission to one another. In Romans 12:3, Paul says, "I say to everyone among you not to think of yourself more highly than you ought to think." In 1 Corinthians 12, Paul chastises the spiritual ones who are claiming Christ's lordship for themselves (vv. 1–3).[6] In Ephesians 4, Paul challenges the believers to humility, gentleness, and patience (vv. 1–2). In each of the gift passages, therefore, we see that Paul requires that all come under Christ's power in all humility, mutually partaking of the gifts for the body. The plurality of the gifts is a practice the undercuts worldly power, the wrong side of power, and makes space for God's power, the right side.

It is best, therefore, to avoid naming anyone "senior pastor" in a church. Those with certain gifts may appear more prominent than others. The apostolic leaders of the church are often the ones taking the lead. They are often out in front. But though they may be first chronologically (1 Cor. 12:28), they are not "over" the church. If we wish to maintain the traditional title of "pastor," apostolic leaders could be called "lead pastor," those who teach called "teaching pastor," and so on. But titles in the church should be redescribed to rid them of any implication of a position over other persons. All things should be done in mutual submission. Even the apostle Paul never exercised his authority over: he refused to usurp, and he called all people who worked with him co-laborers.[7] We should avoid any titles that place a leader over others in the church.

The church, therefore, should be led by a circle of leaders, where Jesus is at the center. Here we can practice the plurality of the gifts in submission to Jesus for the rest of the church to see and follow. The leaders must each know their gifts through a regular process of recognition and affirmation. We lead in mutual submission (as described above) under Christ, recognizing each person's gift and voice. If one has organizational gifts, we empower them to lead out of their gifting. If one has teaching or preaching gifts, we empower them to lead theologically. When big decisions are in play, we gather to pray, listen, and discern. We then encourage the rest of the church, in their house fellowships, in their places of mission, to do the same.

The regular practice of the plurality of the gifts subverts worldly power and makes space for the power of the Holy Spirit to be unleashed by God among us. It is a sign of a church on the right side of power.

Women in Ministry with Men and Godly Power

The practice of women serving alongside men in the church's ordained leadership subverts worldly power and makes space for God's power to work among us. This is because women are different from men, and therefore, by their mere presence as different, they push for a practice of mutuality in leadership. Women, serving with men, call men into mutual submission. Worldly "power over" / patriarchy is undercut, and a space for God to work by His Spirit is opened.

And yet women should be wary. The traditional hierarchical structures of Protestant mainline denominations as well

as the more pragmatic, entrepreneurial hierarchical structures of evangelical megachurches have ordained women
into ministry without any changes to their structures. They,
in essence, invite women into the office of ministry on men's
terms. Women, therefore, find themselves wielding the same
"power over" that men have, with the same consequences on
their characters and the same abuses being foisted on others
that the men have experienced, only somewhat dampened.
In awareness of these dynamics, women in leadership can instead allow their presence to distinguish the powers. Women
can, by their presence and refusal to blend into the structures, disrupt these same structures and the corresponding
cultures if allowed to.

Mainline Protestant churches have traditionally invited
women into ministry on the basis of egalitarian arguments.
Women are equal to men in all ways and therefore should
be included equally into the ranks of clergy. Although the
injustice of inequality is real, this still leaves the hierarchical structures of these institutions in place, alongside the
bad habits of Christendom's alignment with worldly "power
over." Women are invited into an institution encrusted with
male hierarchy and face an uphill struggle to resist becoming molded in the structure that excluded them in the first
place.

Likewise, evangelical churches, culturally driven to reject
the lingering forms of male patriarchy, invite women into
ministry after discovering that Scripture affirms women
in ministry. Coming out from the shadows of John Piper
and Wayne Grudem's *Recovering Biblical Manhood and
Womanhood*,[8] evangelical New Testament scholars write
extensively of the New Testament church's affirmation of
women in ministry. But here again, the "power over" en-
cased in the structures is never addressed. Women are invited into structures of top-down, often celebrity-driven,

leadership. In even more subtle ways, this culture of leadership is sure to pass on to women the malformations of their male predecessors.

Instead, the basis for women entering the ministry of the church alongside men should be the Spirit-filled, charismatic gifts of each leader. Ordination should follow the recognition of the gift and the ensuing manifestation of fruit among the community. This approach should resist initiating all leaders into positions of power over others.[9] Instead, it affirms that the gifts have been poured out among all people, male and female (Acts 2:17). And in a circle of leaders, submitting one to another in the plurality of gifts, there can be no exclusion of women's gifts (or anyone else's) in the leadership of the church. Over years of cultural Christendom, when worldly "power over" was used to organize the church in the place of charismatic authority, women were marginalized.[10] But today the welcoming of women into ministry alongside men can be a practice that makes new space for God's power in the churches. It can be a practice capable of transforming a church from a hierarchy based in "power over" to an engaging relational body infused with godly power capable of connecting to the places where we live. It is evidence of a church on the right side of power.

Conversations

The practice of conversation, of listening to each other, discerning with each other, praying for and with one another, dethrones worldly power and makes space for the power of the Holy Spirit to work among us. Godly power is unleashed. True discipleship happens. And so the church must be more than a Sunday morning gathering of its people. It must cultivate the spaces of conversation that happen in all the places of our lives.

Acts 2:46–47 describes the first believers as gathering at the temple, but also meeting in the social spaces of homes, as well as finding favor connecting with "all the people" in various social spaces where people are not presumed to be believers. The larger central gathering place of worship extends into the other social spaces of life, where conversation happens and where discipleship and mission take place.[11]

Acts 2:42 helpfully summarizes the pattern of conversation as it took place in the life of the believers: "They devoted themselves to the apostles' teaching and fellowship, to the breaking of bread and the prayers." Notice that they ate together (v. 46)—shared in the breaking of bread. Here at the table, where they gather to share a meal, people are equalized. No one is over another person at the table. Worldly "power over" is removed from their midst. This follows the example of Jesus. As Jesus went to be among people, in all sorts of situations, He would migrate to tables, never posturing over (in the Gospel of Luke alone, see 5:27–32; 7:36–50; 9:10–17; 10:38–42; 14:1–24; 19:1–10; 22:14–38; 24:28–43). There is something special about sitting around a table eating that inhibits posturing of oneself over another. It can be the place of presence like no other, where worldly power is disarmed.

Fellowship occurs here. This is not just small talk. This is a way of being together where across this table, as we eat, as we cast our eyes onto the other, we share love, commitment, concern, and a desire to know and be known, all of which is made possible only through the presence of Jesus in this place. By His presence, as we sit together, posturing is overcome. The urges to exert worldly control and power are overcome. We are there in submission one to another.

Acts 2:42 discusses being devoted to the apostles' teaching. So we may study Scripture personally, or we may hear Scripture preached in the Sunday morning gathering, but here around this table is where we flesh out what these texts mean for our lives. For example, in my own house gathering, we read the text from the sermon that week, we ask a question, and then we open the group to discussion. The gifts are alive. We discern how to live. As we submit to the Scriptures together, worldly power is disrupted. We grow.

And then we pray. We submit all things to God in prayer. Prayer, done right, is the giving up of worldly power, the recognition of the holiness and omnipotence of God's work among us ("Holy is your name"). It is the invitation to God to come and work among us ("Thy kingdom come"). And then we petition God, joining in with Him, asking Him to be present in our circumstances, our relationships, and the ongoing struggles of the neighborhood for justice. In this way, the practice of prayer is the ultimate upender of worldly power. It is the way we make space for God to work in and among our lives.

As we gather in my own house gathering every Sunday evening, we follow this simple pattern. As many as fifteen of us gather. We bring food to eat and gather in the kitchen. We say a prayer of thanks and invite the Holy Spirit's real presence into our midst. We sit and listen to each other as we eat. No one talks unless they are asked a question or are asking a question. We are learning how to listen to one another. As the meal winds down, and we sip some decaf coffee, the facilitator reads Scripture from the week's sermon and asks a question. We sit and learn from each other as we discuss and discern people's lives. Occasionally a teacher must instruct, or a pastor must comfort, or a prophet must speak words of clarity. Sometimes an issue is so intense in a person's life that the conversation must continue in a one-on-one time with someone. As the time winds down, we submit all concerns, all our neighbors, the problems in our town, to the reigning Lord in prayer.

Miracles happen here. Key justice issues of the community are raised here. In my experience, churches have worked best when the big decisions for the church start here. Here they are discerned out of everyday life. In the most organic of ways, issues flow from here to the leaders and back in a flow of mutuality. When a church flows only from the top down, existing Christians may comply, but those needing discipleship and those noticing injustice issues that lie deep in a place get missed. Conversations around the table stir discipleship and space for the Spirit to work. They are a sign of a church living on the right side of power.

Multiethnic Church

The segregated church is a remnant of worldly power. It gathers people efficiently into homogeneous spaces of hegemonic worldly power. It organizes people to be readily comfortable in the status quo, with less conflict. In the past, when White-majority churches marginalized Black persons in the United States, Black persons could not sit in the main congregation, and they were monitored regarding their teachings on the Bible (and slavery). As a result, Black communities had to organize their own churches (as well as colleges). Black church was built to survive White supremacy, a manifestation of worldly power. Many years later, multiethnic church is a viable practice of protest and resistance to these worldly powers.

And yet we must be wary here as well. For if the multiethnic church is organized from the top down, using worldly "power over"—even with the best of intentions—it will be multiethnic in appearance only. It may have a diverse leadership, worship team, and even congregation, but it will still be a majority-culture space. The ethnic group most in power will govern the church. This is how we get ethnic churches, led by non-White persons, strangely organized to be cultural White-majority spaces.

Korie Edwards, in her fascinating study of a multiethnic church in *The Elusive Dream*, describes the ways an intentionally multicultural church failed to escape the hegemony of Whiteness. Despite the church leadership being Black persons, their decisions on worship, on the kinds of sermons to be preached, and on the kinds of programs to run were driven by a desire to meet the needs of the majority White persons. It is the White persons in the church who had the most affluence, who gave the church the most financial support, who had the most mobility, and who could leave any time they chose to in order to pursue their consumerist needs at another church. The church therefore catered to the White persons. And so this multiethnic church, with a diverse congregation, ended up being White culturally, with a Black pastor. The pastor, Edwards says, "was embedded in a structure that dictated that people in positions of power affirm white evangelical culture."[12]

Edwards exposes the many ways hierarchies function in multiethnic churches. She discusses leadership in the church in terms of pastors, up-front paid staff, how worship decisions are made, the hiring of pastors, how pastors lead, the pressures they face. It is all an exposure of "power over" and the work it does to undermine true multiethnic church. In this specific church there were no signs of house fellowships, smaller groups, any ongoing practices of conversation, fellowship with or tending to one another, reconciliation, prayer, sharing life, or discipleship practices.

And so if multiethnic church is truly to be multiethnic, if it is to be a work of the Spirit amid the confluence of cultural forces meeting in a social space to live under Christ's power, if it is not to be another expression of the majority culture with a little more ethnic diversity, the church must be organized on the foundation of local, smaller discipleship spaces of conversation. Here, where people of diverse ethnicities gather around a table and listen and discern, decisions are made, revelations received, understandings revealed, generating actual relational transformation to then influence the community at large. All the things that make up church, including sermon topics, music style, issues to be discerned, and programs to be led, arise from the bottom up. A culture of cultures is miraculously formed as a witness to what God can do through godly power at work among a gathered people.

The practice of multiethnic church, therefore, must be centered and organized from the bottom up, from the local to the big. It must be founded in smaller and multiple spaces of conversation where godly power by the Spirit can work to make all things new. Then and only then does a multiethnic church become a church that upends the worldly power and lives on the right side of power.

The IGTHSUS Meeting

When a conflict or a theological disagreement happens among the members of a church, typically it is those in power who solve the conflict. The teaching pastor sets forth the official position, usually in a congregational meeting, and the matter is settled. He (most often a "he") goes into his office, as Moses went to Mount Sinai, studies the Bible, hears from the Lord, and then, like Moses coming down from the mountain, delivers the edict. The congregation is to comply. Those who disagree leave. This is all done in the ways of worldly power over.

The alternative is for the leaders to call an IGTHSUS meeting, a meeting that emerges from below, undercuts worldly power, and makes space for the Spirit to work among us. The practice of IGTHSUS takes its pattern from the process outlined in Acts 15. The name IGTHSUS, adopted by my own church, takes its acrostic letters from the phrase "it has seemed good to the Holy Spirit and to us" (v. 28), a phrase appearing in the middle of the letter sent by "the apostles and the elders, with the consent of the whole church" (v. 22), to the gentile believers to express the resolution of the conflict.

In Acts 15, a conflict emerges over whether new gentile believers must be required to keep the Jewish law and to be circumcised (v. 5). The issue had gained importance across the church as a whole. Likewise, in our church, when a conflict or disagreement does not meet resolution in one of our local house gatherings and the issue itself gains importance to the church community at large, it is time to call an IGTHSUS meeting. Such a conflict or disagreement usually starts locally in discipleship. As with Matthew 18:15–20, when a conflict is not resolved, more of our members get invited to discern together. If the issue gains in importance, so that the community at large is asking for guidance, it should be the practice of a church to call an IGTHSUS meeting. Notice however, that the move of the Spirit starts in smaller gatherings and moves to the whole, not vice versa.

In Acts 15, the leaders—the apostles and the elders—meet to consider whether the issue is of broader importance to the community (Acts 15:6). When they decided it reached a certain importance, they called a meeting of all those in the community interested in devoting themselves to discerning the issue. Likewise, at our church, it is customary to invite all those interested in the issue and willing to devote prayer and much time (possibly several meetings) in mutual submission to listen, reflect, and discern for the church as a whole (v. 12).

In Acts 15, the community hears from the experiences of people. What has the Holy Spirit been doing in people's lives around this issue? What has been the fruit in people's lives surrounding this issue (Acts 15:8–9, 12)? The community hears from the teachers on what Scripture has to say on the matter (vv. 15–19). We do likewise in our church. We have found it is important to hear from those who differ in the interpretation of Scripture. We must take questions and hear not only differing interpretations but from where each person learned the interpretation and what were the key influences of the interpretation, including past preachers and past experiences. We must come to see Scripture with fresh eyes for this moment at hand.

In Acts 15, there comes a moment of unity when "it has seemed good to the Holy Spirit and to us" to articulate the agreement for all to share and agree on. Likewise, in our church, after much prayer, the leaders discern a statement that summarizes the consensus. This statement must faithfully extend the gospel and scriptural wisdom into the situation. The statement is presented to the discerning community, and everyone is surveyed using a gradient from 1 to 5. One extreme of the gradient—the number 1—signals a veto. A person responding with a 1 sees the statement as evil and from Satan and cannot participate in affirming it in any way. This is the most grievous of opinions to be discerned among the group. The other extreme of the gradient—the number 5—signals wholehearted agreement with the statement, with no reservation. The person choosing the number 4 signals that they are not yet convinced but that they now trust and see the Holy Spirit at work in this community and can support the consensus of this community.

One time, when discerning whether our congregation ought to have women pastors, we received all 5s, except for two 4s. The two 4s said they could follow the community's leading since they had seen the Spirit visibly at work in the process. One of the two persons had been experiencing bad headaches for months, and after the final meeting, those headaches were now gone. I mention this to illustrate how the community came to peace over the issue and moved forward even when there was unanimity.

The IGTHSUS meeting is where people with voices are concretely heard, where actual situations in people's lives are reflected on, where accounts of the working of the Holy Spirit are recognized, where bad fruit is exposed, where good fruit is seen, where persons are known. It is an upending of worldly "power over." It is a practice of making space for God's power to work among us. If the issue that is discerned bears forth fruit in the community, the community will flourish. If the issue is discerned out of bad faith, the community will shrink and die.

If the issue becomes a broad, sweeping cultural issue across many churches in a denomination, these local discernments, and the fruit that comes from them, should bear testimony to denominational leadership at large. As always, the movement should move from the local, grassroots IGTHSUS meetings across the country up to the denominational level, where testimonies can be heard and the church at large can say, "It seems good to the Holy Spirit and to us." But it must come from the ground up, in submission to godly power at work through the Spirit, not worldly power imposed from the top down. This is how God transforms churches, denominations, and the world: from the right side of God's power.

Discerning Sexuality

No issue has stirred up more consternation among Christians today than the discernment of LGBTQ sexuality in the life of the church. Churches and denominations have split over whether to affirm or not affirm LGBTQ sexuality as normative for the Christian faith. The decision "to affirm" usually includes the endorsement of same-sex marriage and the ordination of LGBTQ clergy. It is perhaps the single most divisive issue among Christians. And yet discerning sexuality could also be a powerful practice of godly power manifesting God's healing presence among hurting and marginalized persons.

Regrettably, the majority of churches/denominations opt for exercising worldly power in the key moments of discerning sexuality. Even though the leaders attempt to hear from all voices, the decision is almost always delivered in the form of a policy statement, implemented from the presiding officers, over church members or member churches of the denomination. The edict comes in such a sweeping nature, affirming or not affirming all LGBTQ sexuality / gender identity, that it sweeps aside numerous issues at the core of modern sexuality, leaving little space for God to work in the lives of His people, no matter what sexuality they identify with.

Such policy statements, by definition, group people's sexuality/gender struggles into one large category—LGBTQ— while saying little about what Christian marriage is or is not, what attraction is, and what role attraction should play in our lives. Likewise, these policy statements say little about what defines male/female or other. Attraction and desire are assumed to be univocal. Gender constructs are assumed to be as given by the respective culture.

Yet attraction in our society is diverse. The most prominent of queer theorists alert us to how misogyny, sexualization of bodies, and even patriarchy are justified via "it is just the way I'm attracted to someone." Attraction is naturalized. The average person today is aware of toxic masculinity and how it has invaded certain parts of evangelical Christianity. But at times, attraction toward "hot wives" in these churches is seen as natural. We need safe spaces where we can discern our attractions, where they come from, what role they play in our lives, how attraction works, and how it grows in good ways over time or is malformed within toxic frameworks. Heterosexuals should be the first ones in line for these discernments.

God not only wants to work for healing in our sexual lives and our gendered existence; He wants to transform our cultures of sexuality and gender. But if we simply endorse attraction generally by affirming, or not affirming, all LGBTQ attractions, if we affirm all transgender identities without any examination of the male-female binaries that such transitions assume and that may indeed be toxic, we are in essence affirming the attractions / gender binaries as they are given by our existing church culture or the culture at large. We smooth over many of the most important personal discernments of people's lives having to do with sexuality and gender and turn them into an ideologized position. This, I contend, is the way control, coercion, and "power over" works. And it removes any space for God to work among us by the power of the Holy Spirit.

Ideology is a tool of worldly power. Ideology works by taking an issue people are dealing with in their daily lives, extracting it, and making it into a flag that can be waved to enlist people for or against it. People are depersonalized. And those in worldly power can control and rally people to their causes and hold on to power. In the process, people's real lives are glossed over. Real-life issues are not examined. And the bitter antagonisms that arise and divide people in anger against or for the issue leave no space for God by the Holy Spirit to work. "Power over" prohibits the real work God wants to do in our lives and in our world regarding sexuality and gender.[13]

Today, the church, which has been largely unwilling to talk about sex, can no longer pontificate its way out of this crisis. It must cultivate safe places, intimate spaces, of conversation, where people can unwind the angers, the pains, the abuses, the resentments of marginalization. These places require examination of the frames of gender binaries and sexuality stereotypes that have been handed down to us, in some cases by our culture, but endorsed by the church, only in exclusionist terms. We need spaces for the Holy Spirit to speak and work healing. It is time for the church to take care of her children and of the wounded ones who have been shunned by her pathetic lack of sexual discipleship.

We need churches with the courage to hold the spaces open, resisting the move to ideological foreclosure of the space by not-affirming / affirming policy statements. These churches must provide a way to say something to all those persons who have been abused by the church's attempts to use worldly "power over" to enforce a sexuality/gender construct without conversation, discussion, examination, discernment. Those persons must know they are seen, they are loved, they are accepted, they are God's children, they are welcome.

Instead of a policy statement enforced over people, a discipleship process should be offered, and it should be offered to everyone equally and inclusively, and heterosexuals should get in line first. All are invited to live into what God is doing under His power, the power of the resurrected Lord among us to heal and restore our sexual and gendered lives.

There may come a time for an IGTHSUS meeting, but we will not rush. God the Holy Spirit is at work among us through Her people. And when we do have some understandings and wisdom to apply to the church as a whole, or to a denomination as a whole, it will come from the reports of real persons' lives. We will offer practices of discipleship through the power and presence of the living Christ, not rules to be enforced over people's lives. These will be the signs we are living on the right side of power.

The Practice of *Parrhēsia*

Telling the truth is a practice of the Christian life. Telling the truth in a certain way undermines worldly power and makes way for the power of God through His Spirit to become manifest among us. The New Testament sometimes speaks of this practice with the Greek word *parrhēsia*.

Parrhēsia in the New Testament, as understood within various Greco-Roman contexts of the time, refers to speaking the truth in relationship, with sincerity, no malice, out of concern and love for persons and a love for the truth. It is spoken out of genuine presence with someone, with a group of people. It is embodied. Not detached. It is spoken as lived truth. The truth that one says can be witnessed to in one's actual life. It is on display. Speaking truth in this way always risks total transparency. It puts one's own well-being on the line. Speaking truth in this way is often evidenced by the fact that the person speaking has much to lose in saying it. In all these ways, *parrhēsia* is a specific practice of speaking truth to power that disrupts worldly power.

In modern American politics, we have become used to thinking about truth in the abstract, as something that can be debated or proven with evidence. Belief in the truth is separated from the truth. We extract the truth from everyday lived life as something to be examined in order to determine whether the mind should assent to it and believe it. But with *parrhēsia* there is no such Cartesian separation of truth from life. Truth is already proven in the living. One verbalizes it in order to give witness to it. It is impossible to separate truth from my belief in it inasmuch as I, the one saying it, am already living it.

There can therefore be no violence or malice in such *parrhēsia*. The person speaking truth is strangely at peace in a very present sort of way. With *parrhēsia* truth is never used as a weapon to manipulate circumstances. The person, in the act of speaking truth, actually gives up control, becoming vulnerable within his or her life. *Parrhēsia* actually transforms the person speaking into a witness to the truth in body and soul. There is an almost supernatural patience about it because of the speaker's confidence that the truth can speak for itself.[14]

For all these reasons, the very practice of *parrhēsia* undercuts worldly power. It is disruptive to the existing order. So compelling is this truth that it cannot be denied. It causes people to question the existing ideologies that they are held captive in. Through *parrhēsia*, space is opened up for God's power to work. The Spirit can then lead into all truth (John 16:13). This truth, both spoken and lived, can then be used by God for His purposes.

This is such a different kind of speech act than what we are used to seeing in the world. It is why "revivals" break out when people start confessing their sin and speaking truth. Their lives are exposed, they give up worldly power, and they allow God's Spirit to fill the room. It is why worldly power, the grab for control and power over, the saving of face at all cost, squelch God's power and unleash the ways of abuse. It is why social activism on Twitter cannot accomplish much because it so often detaches the truth from the one speaking truth and in turn weaponizes it to get more clicks, more worldly power, within the algorithms of social media.

As we live in the world of fake news, Twitter storms, conspiracy theories, and political antagonisms, we are tempted to doubt whether truth can even be possible in a way that changes the world. But, as philosopher/cultural theorist Michel Foucault argued, *parrhēsia* is powerful political speech. In a lecture series on *parrhēsia* delivered at the University of California, Berkeley, he showed that truth telling can have a profoundly subversive, revolutionary impact down through history.[15]

Certainly we should be careful not to overlap too easily Foucault's study of *parrhēsia*'s political effects with the use of the word in the New Testament. Nonetheless, in the New Testament we do see evidence of the social effects *parrhēsia* can have when used by the Spirit. In Acts 4, for instance, Peter and John have been arrested for proclaiming Jesus. They are brought before the rulers, elders, scribes, and high priests—all those who hold worldly power in their firm grasp (vv. 5–6). At full risk to themselves, Peter and John speak truth. When the rulers see the *parrhēsia* with which the apostles speak (v. 13), when they recognize that the detainees are ordinary, uneducated men and followers of Jesus, when they see the one who was cured standing beside them, they can say nothing in opposition to them. They are stunned. They let Peter and John go, with orders to be quiet (v. 18), but they cannot stop them by worldly power (vv. 20–21).

The believers got together and prayed for more unstoppable *parrhēsia* (v. 29). They praised God, inhabited His reign, were filled with the Holy Spirit, and spoke the word of God with more *parrhēsia* (v. 31). And a social revolution began. It is all an example of how the practice of *parrhēsia* working and how speaking truth as Christians put us on the right side of power.

Embodied Presence in Public Demonstrations

Public demonstration can be a practice of godly power. Christians join with others to present themselves bodily, relationally, socially and to speak truth as embodied presence. We put our very bodies in the way of evil, giving witness with our presence to another power at work.[16] This opens space for so much more than a preservative act of justice. We seek changes to the relational social realities of people's lives. True embodied presence disrupts the very hold of worldly "power over" that keeps unjust systems in place. When combined with the practice of *parrhēsia*, it opens space for godly power to work. A new world can be born in the Spirit. This is how Christians go into the world.

A midsized city in Arizona, like so many other cities in North America, was experiencing an opioid epidemic. The number of overdoses and deaths was increasing month to month. A few pastors, working together with social activists, started discussions around their city proposing to establish an opioid treatment facility in the downtown core, where so many addicts were.

These pastors held teaching sessions around the city in churches and community centers. They spoke as persons having done numerous funerals for opioid overdose victims, as having family members, church members, and street acquaintances who had died from opioid overdose. They spoke truth out of walking with those suffering with opioid addiction. In other words, they spoke with *parrhēsia*. They set up information booths in churches, training people how to use Alloxan kits to reverse overdose. The city rallied around the cause. The treatment site was approved by the state government. Everything was in place. The whole community was behind it.

But then, a few months later, right before the center was to be opened, a new city council was voted in. A newly elected councilman put forth a motion to deny support for the center. Other newer council members joined with him. They argued that drug addicts need to be arrested not enabled. The treatment center's existence was now in severe jeopardy. Word got around town. Three of the pastors organized a demonstration. An embodied demonstration of several hundred people gathered around city hall on the morning of the council meeting to decide on the motion to deny funding for the center. Anger toward the council members was stirring in the crowd. Violence was imminent.

And then one of the pastors got up to speak, put his hand over his heart, and asked everyone in the crowd who had lost a family member or a friend to opioid addiction to put their hand over their heart. The crowd calmed. They stood embodied in solidarity with the truth of their cause. A prayer was offered up. The embodied, peaceful, sincere speech of *parrhēsia* opened space for God to work. The council meeting that followed dropped the motion to deny the funding before there was any debate.

A few hours later, the activists and pastors were celebrating "the victory" on the second level of a local bar. The council members—who had originally sponsored the motion against the treatment facility—were down below on the first floor. An activist came upstairs and told everyone that he had just hurled a string of expletives at the council members, putting them in their place, for their outrageous motion against the persons of this town. The pastors looked deflated in response. "We're not here to demonize anyone," they said. "We're here to build relationships, keep conversation going (the job is not done with legislation)." In a practice of *parrhēsia*, the violence was quelled. One of the council members came up without any prompting and said that the people of the town needed to be a family in this. Families often disagree, but the members of this family needed healing and a return to working together for the community.

An hour or so later, one of the social activists came up to one of the pastors and said that he had long ago rejected the church and Christianity. He saw it as fake, hypocritical, and damaging to people. He could not imagine that Christians even cared about people who were hurting. And so he asked, "Does your church baptize people? For the first time in years I feel drawn to Jesus and want to know him in my life."

This true story (some details changed to hide identities) illustrates how the practice of *parrhēsia* works in embodied demonstration. Such embodied demonstration makes space for so much more than a piece of legislation (or the refusal of such). It makes space for a healing and reconciled new social reality to be born out of God's power at work drawing people to Himself. People's lives are not only preserved through a center for treatment of opioid addiction; they are also restored. Relationships between people divided by politics are healed. Those who hurt are united with those in a better place who can come alongside them. A new kingdom social space emerges that few people could have imagined. And in the process people are brought into Christ's kingdom. Embodied demonstrations like these put the church on the right side of power.

More Than a Social Justice Project

As the previous story illustrates, the local church's work of justice, under the auspices of godly power, can do more than preserve minimal procedural justice. It can be used to change the world. It can do more than preserve lives; it can transform lives in Christ's kingdom. But too often the local church settles for organizing what I'll label "social justice projects."

Injustice inhabits the worlds around our church gatherings. There is racism, homeless populations struggling to survive, a neighborhood lacking a grocery store, a school lacking enough resources to provide needed textbooks and computers for students, a minority population that is unseen when met with police brutality. The church seeks to respond. It may seek to provide basic needs for homeless persons, a soup kitchen once a week, textbooks for a school, a demonstration of solidarity with minority populations suffering racism. By volunteer organizing, using political leverage, giving money to bring resources, creating political restraints upon further violence, we can intervene with worldly power. It is all the good work of preserving people's lives.

But we are called into more.

By also being present to the spaces that are opened up relationally, between people, between gatherings of people, we can generate conversations, opportunities for prayer, opportunities to invite people into the practice of actual repentance, reconciliation, and restoration. In these spaces that are opened, there are opportunities for the practice of *parrhēsia*, praying for healing, sitting around tables; a neighborhood can be changed, a new world under God's reign can be born. What starts out as an act of organizing a justice project can turn into an outbreak of the Holy Spirit if we can just be present on the right side of power.

One time, in a city I know, a city ordinance committee in a suburb decided not to allow a restaurant into town. The suburb's population, once largely blue-collar White persons, was changing, and this was a famous Black-owned restaurant known for its fish and chicken in the Black communities of this large city. The village commissioner openly said on the record that this restaurant would bring in "the wrong kind of people." It was a brazenly racist statement. Outrage was expressed. Eventually the ordinance was changed. Ten years later a restaurant entered town that was much loved by the Black populations new to the town. But there was much more work to be done. A simple invitation by some church members on that village committee to the commissioner with some Black friends over a cup of coffee, praying for God to work, could have been the space for God to open minds, convict persons of their sin, and work together for a new way of being together.

Some church people in that town, however, thought that the job was done when the ordinance was changed. After the hard work of changing the law was finished, no one invited the city manager to the table of fellowship, sharing a beverage, with persons of color, praying for God's Spirit to work around that table. The work of justice in regard to that ordinance was important, but there is so much more God wants to do to heal, transform, and change the way people love each other, cooperate, and live together. If we would make space for God's power to work, we need an imagination for justice that pushes beyond preservative works of justice. God is calling local churches, under the auspices of His power, to do more than another social justice project. This is what it means to be a church on the right side of power.

Evangelism and Mission

Evangelism is a practice of godly power, a manifestation of the presence of the power of God. Since the Great Awakenings, however, techniques of evangelism have often been coercive, manipulative, based on fear and inducing guilt. Modern techniques such as evangelism explosion and comic book tracts that scare people with hell answer questions before they are asked. These techniques then become tools of coercion used to manipulate conversions. Such control and manipulation are the signs of an evangelism taken in by worldly power. It is colonialism of a different kind, and in a culture that is post-Christendom, such techniques stir resentment. As a result, evangelism has become a despised practice both within and outside the church in North America.

Evangelism, however, should be the opposite of control and manipulation. It should be the practice of presence in people's lives, discerning what the Spirit is doing in people's lives drawing them to God in Christ. It should be a practice of submission to God and His power at work all around us.

So instead of going door to door in the neighborhood with a friend doing an evangelism explosion survey on unsuspecting people, instead of having a movie night at the church building where we scare unsuspecting people with the *Thief in the Night* movie, instead of trying to convince someone that they might get hit by a car and go into an eternity in hell and deserve it, we ought to go out into our villages—as Jesus sends us—to sit at tables with persons of peace sharing food or a beverage (Luke 10:7). The harvest is already grown and ready to be harvested (v. 2). We do not need to use human power. Instead, we sit as a guest, eating what is set before us (vv. 7–8). Bringing no money (v. 4), we give up worldly control and power. We stay in one place in the neighborhood (v. 7). We do not quickly move on unless completely rejected. We are present. We are listening. We are waiting on what God is doing to be revealed.

When someone reveals their pain, their hurt, their confusion, their lostness, we pray for them. When they are healed (Luke 10:9) or illumined, we respond by giving witness: "I believe that is my God who is working in you." The kingdom of His lordship is breaking in (v. 9). We ask, "Are you interested?" Jesus's power is unleashed. Satan's power is dismantled (v. 18). *Dynameis* (acts of power) are released under the authority (*exousia*) of Jesus (v. 19). Nonetheless, it is not something we did in control of worldly power. We are truly only participants in God's power, as persons with our names written in heaven (v. 20).

And so we must train ourselves to do something so foreign to our age, and to the evangelism strategies of times past: be present in the hurting places where we live, sit at tables with people, listen, be regular, allow space for the Spirit to work. Know how to ask questions, speak truth sincerely, offer reconciliation, invite people into the kingdom, invite them to accept Jesus as Lord over our lives, our towns, allowing Him to use His wonder-working power in their lives. This kind of evangelism is the mark of a church on the right side of power.

Will We Sow the Seed? Becoming a People on the Right Side of Power

And so we end with this question: Will we sow the seed of God's subversive revolution on the right side of God's power, His Holy Spirit–breathed power? Will we sow the seeds of godly power through these practices (and more)?

Like the seed that falls on the rocky ground, some of these practices will find no soil to take root. Look for the fertile soil. And like the seed that gets snatched away by the birds, some of these practices will be given up on when they barely get started. Teach patience. And like the seed that sprouts quickly but doesn't have roots, some of these practices will get initial excitement but quickly die. Push for going deeper. Unfortunately, many will reject the ways of God's power (the parable suggests at least three out of four) for the power of the world. Nonetheless, it is in these ways that we slowly make space for the King and His subversive transforming kingdom. Slowly we become a people on the right side of His power, instead of people bent on living on the wrong side of worldly power. Then one day a church or a house fellowship explodes with manifestations of the Spirit, transformed lives, and a demonstration of God's justice in the neighborhood. A few more people catch the fire of the Spirit. And God's revolution begins.

In the meantime, do not be discouraged. In the words of the great Oscar Romero, "Let us not be disheartened as though human realities made impossible the accomplishment of God's plans."[17] We who seek to live under God's power cannot be in control. All will happen under His power in good time.

EPILOGUE

We Can Be a Different People;
Getting Back on the Right Side of Power

> I pray . . . you may know . . . what is the immeasurable greatness of his power for us who believe. . . . God put this power to work in Christ when he raised him from the dead and seated him at his right hand in the heavenly places, far above all rule and authority and power and dominion.
>
> Ephesians 1:17–21

The Church on the Wrong Side of History

The church is regularly accused of being on the wrong side of history. In America the White church was slow to work for justice in regard to slavery and racism, women's rights, women in ministry, social justice, and alleviating poverty in our culture. In each case, it was late to the fight, jumping on the bandwagon for justice long after the culture at large was beating the drum. In the same manner, the argument goes, the church is late on working for justice regarding LGBTQ peoples.[1] Again and again, the church, it seems, doesn't lead history but follows it. And it is regularly, if not always, on the wrong side of it.

This phrase "the right side of history" has been part of America's moral vocabulary for decades. Most prominently, Martin Luther King Jr. used it in his speeches, having borrowed the term from the abolitionist Theodore Parker. Presidents Reagan and Clinton were fond of it. President Barack Obama used "the right side of history," or its converse, "the wrong side of history," twenty-eight times in major speeches.[2] Underlying the phrase in all these usages was the conviction that "the arc of history bends toward justice" and we must join in.[3]

The church, as well, is urged to get on the right side of history. A century ago, following in the spirit of Hegel and Marx, American Protestants believed that inherent progress (called a dialectic) was built into history. Mainline Protestants were postmillennialists, believing that the kingdom of God had been set loose into history. Walter Rauschenbusch—to name one paragon of this theology—preached that the kingdom of God had entered history in Jesus.[4] The church's job, therefore, is to enlist Christians into this march of history for justice. The church, Rauschenbusch said, needed to cooperate with bringing the whole world toward the justice at work in these historical processes set loose in the kingdom of God.[5]

And yet, despite these voices, the church has still regularly failed to be on the right side of this history.

Wrong Side of History or Wrong Side of Power?

A closer look at recent American history, however, offers an alternative prognosis. If we look closely at these historical moments, each time White Christians in America sided with proslavery, patriarchal, and exploitive economic practices—

in other words, with the wrong side of history—they were occupying a place of privilege, aligned with worldly power, money, class, and status. That is, following the theme of this book, the church was on the wrong side of power. Aligned with worldly power, the church acted to guard the status quo.

On the other hand, when Christians were present among the marginalized, oppressed, and powerless (in terms of worldly power), space was opened up, God moved in the power of the Spirit, and the church led the world for justice. And so, more often than not, when the church found itself on the wrong side of history, the problem was not only that the church was on the wrong side of history but that it was on the wrong side of power.

Christians, situated among the powerless (not possessing worldly power) and their churches, became the instigators of the abolitionist, feminist, poverty-alleviating transformative movements. They were not perfect. Some were racists. They were still constantly tempted to blur the powers. But by and large, the church that ended up on the right side of history working for justice—that, in fact, led that history—was the church first postured under the power of God at work among the poor.

If the church, therefore, desires to discern God's justice, it should not seek to first discern where history is going at any given time, and then try to get on the right side of it. Instead, it should first seek a posture among the oppressed, the (worldly) powerless. Here God's power by the Spirit can be discerned and joined in with. The church that seeks to be on the right side of godly power will be on the right side of history.

Claiming "the right side of history" can itself be a "power move," seeking to leverage worldly power.[6] Instead of doing that, the church should resist siding with worldly power when at all possible. Be present among the powerless (in worldly terms), freed from the control and coercion of the oppressions and ideologies of worldly power. Here we can discern God's power at work and join with Him in the work He is already doing. We will be cautious about, if not averse to, availing ourselves of the powers of worldly coercion and control, and instead pursue the relational, convicting, healing, reconciling power of the risen Christ at work in and among people. This is the lesson of being on the right side of history. We must first be on the right side of God's power.

This pattern has been illustrated in the history of the much-despised White evangelicalism of North America, often seen as being on the wrong side of history. Through historians Jemar Tisby and Donald Dayton we see that actually, evangelicals were on the wrong side of history when they were on the wrong side of power. When they were on the right side of power, amazing works of justice came forth.

Jemar Tisby

In *The Color of Compromise*, Jemar Tisby details the White church's complicity with slavery. One of his main contentions is, "White complicity with racism isn't a matter of melanin, it's a matter of power. . . . Whether society is stratified according to class, gender, religion, or tribe, communities tend to put power in the hands of a few to the detriment of many. In the United States, power runs along color lines, and white people have the most influence."[7] Tisby shows how, over time, several Christian church leaders who started out working against the horrors of slavery in eighteenth-century America turned toward accepting and even endorsing slavery.

Tisby, I believe, is describing a drifting of the White churches from the right side of God's power to the wrong side of (worldly) power. They blurred the two powers.

George Whitefield (1714–70), for example, under the influence of John Wesley, "excoriated enslavers" for the way they treated slaves. As he preached among the lower classes, revivals broke out, and Whitefield became a critic of the practice of slavery in America. He started out among the poor, on the right side of God's power. Spurred by Wesley, Whitefield then built what became the Bethesda Orphanage in Savannah, Georgia, a noble cause aimed at providing support to orphans in the South. It was this Whitefield, postured among the (worldly) powerless, who worked to rid the world of slavery.

But this orphanage bordered on financial ruin. So Whitefield joined with some wealthy allies in South Carolina to keep it going. They bought land, started a plantation, and hoped to sustain the orphanage through the profits of the plantation. The plantation, however, struggled to make a profit. To compete, the plantation required slaves to make it profitable. And so, stunningly, Whitefield became a leader in petitioning the state legislature of Georgia, a free territory, to allow slavery. Aligned with the forces of moneymaking and worldly power, the famed revivalist blurred the powers and lost his ability to discern God's justice.[8] Tisby describes how Whitefield's critique of slavery morphed into outright support for slavery. Whitefield, perhaps with the good intentions of supporting an orphanage, nonetheless went over to the wrong side of power. In doing so he ended up on the wrong side of history.

Jonathan Edwards (1703–58) was a supporter of slavery. Tisby suggests that his support of slavery may, in part, be attributed to his social status. He pastored a wealthy and influential congregation where slave-owning signified status. His theology focused on individual conversion and piety, so he could avoid the social, systemic issue of slavery as superfluous to salvation. His son Jonathan Edwards Jr., however, was different. He was sent at the age of ten by his father to live among the Mahican and Mohawk tribes and learn their languages in order to be a missionary. He spoke their languages better than English as a boy. Jonathan Jr., who lived among these oppressed people at the time, became an abolitionist. Able to see and resist the ways of worldly power, he ended up on the right side of history. His father, on the wrong side of worldly power, ended up on the wrong side of history.[9]

John Wesley (1703–91) himself found slavery appalling. Although he was far from advocating for racial equality, his antislavery stance—along with his emphasis on revivalism, interracial camp meetings, a swift ordination process, and an appeal to the non-elite classes—initially attracted Black Christians. But as the denomination grew and reached up into higher echelons of establishment wealth and power, it became more accommodating to slavery, depending on where the churches were located. Tisby details the splits that happened among both the Methodists and the Baptists a hundred years after the Great Awakening revivals. Denominations located in the South, where money and power were aligned with slavery, became the center of proslavery justifications. Churches in the North—where, because of industrialization, slavery had become a nonissue for economic power—became abolitionist.[10] The proslavery positions of churches were not only on the wrong side of history; they were dug in on the wrong side of worldly power.

Even in more recent history, White evangelicalism's alignments with worldly power have led to it being on the wrong side of the struggles for justice in North America. Tisby details carefully the origins of today's Religious Right with Billy Graham and his relationship with Richard Nixon and the beginnings of "the Southern Strategy."[11] This strategy sought to develop certain "law and order" policies to appeal to White voters who were afraid of movements to integrate the Black peoples of America into full citizenship in society. It is stunning how this alignment with the power of government, worldly power, polluted the judgment of Christians, preventing them from seeing what God was doing in relation to civil rights, racial reconciliation, and the shaping of a more just world.

Tisby's work, therefore, shows us that when the church is on the wrong side of history's struggles for justice, you can usually count on it being on the wrong side of worldly power.

Donald Dayton

Donald Dayton, a historian of evangelicalism, has long argued that North American evangelicalism originated within the Holiness revivals among the poor of the 1800s, not the wealthy Princeton Reformed Inerrantists of a similar time. Those revivalists lived among, ministered among, and advocated for the poor, the marginalized, the oppressed. They were on the right side of (godly) power.

Dayton examines Wheaton College, a modern-day symbol of evangelicalism, whose president was the avowed abolitionist Jonathan Blanchard (1811–92). Blanchard sponsored the Underground Railroad, which ran through Wheaton College's main building (known today as Blanchard Hall). Many of the enslaved hid there in its tunnels on their way to freedom. Dayton highlights the famous Cincinnati Abolition Society, where Blanchard debated the gradualist N. L. Rice on the abolition of slavery, speaking against the forces of the "religion of the privileged class." In terms of his abolitionism, Blanchard was on the right side of history. But prior to that, he lived and worked from a posture among the poor, on the right side of power, godly power.[12]

Dayton details how Charles Finney (1792–1875) left the auspices of his Old School Presbyterianism of Princeton to start a New School Presbyterianism at Oberlin College. Finney rejected going to the wealthy and prestigious Princeton Theological Seminary. He intentionally cultivated a church among the lower classes (his churches in New York were known for their "free pews," which welcomed the poor). This led Finney to later embrace the emerging Holiness movement and its anti-hierarchical social philosophy.[13] From here Finney led Oberlin College, the hotbed of abolitionism, a school that trained many of the new leaders of the movement such as Theodore Weld and Blanchard. In contrast to Charles Hodge's support of slavery from the wealthy halls of Princeton, Finney spurred the abolitionist movements from his more humble abode at Oberlin. Although there were surely mixed motivations and some enduring racism among these abolitionists, their trajectory toward abolition came from a rejection of the worldly power of the predominant culture. They lived and discerned from the right side of godly power.

Dayton's work outlines how it was the Holiness movements, the revivals, and, indeed, the Pentecostal movements, among the poor, where the work for the abolition of slavery, the emancipation of women into equal participation in church leadership, and the work of alleviating poverty among the poor was done by the Salvation Army, the Nazarenes, the Christian and Missionary Alliance, Free Methodists, Wesleyan Methodists, and many more. These movements were not perfect. In all these movements there were mixed motives, sometimes overtones of White supremacy, sometimes attitudes of "separate but equal."[14] Nonetheless, where there was a presence and a posture of with-ness among the poor and the oppressed, there was a push forward toward justice regarding slaves, women, and the poor.

In a fascinating section at the end of Dayton's book *Rediscovering an Evangelical Heritage*, he explores the difference between Charles Hodge and Princeton's Old Calvinism, on

the one hand, and Charles Finney and his New Holiness–
driven Presbyterianism. The first supported slavery as an
institution and worked against women in leadership/voting
and equal rights. The second seeded the abolitionist movement and avid support for women's suffrage and women in
leadership and ministry. Over time, however, Holiness Movement evangelicalism was replaced by the influence of Prince-
tonian Old Calvinism, which focused on belief over practice
and on defense of the Bible over engagement with social ills.
"What had begun as a Christian egalitarianism was transformed into a type of Christian elitism. Revivalistic currents
that had once been bent to the liberation of the slave now
allied themselves with wealth and power against the civil
rights movement. Churches and movements that had once
pioneered a new role for women became the most resistant
to contemporary movements seeking the same goals."[15] It was
not that evangelicalism suddenly moved to the wrong side of
history. It was that evangelicalism had slowly moved from
the side of godly power to the side of worldly power—the
wrong side of power.

Dayton shows how Holiness movements from the 1800s
moved repeatedly, almost naturally, to improved socio-
economics. He calls this trend the "embourgeoisement" of
evangelicalism.[16] Holiness congregations moved from being
among the lower strata of society to being among the middle
and upper classes as their lives were saved from alcoholism,
brokenness, and lack of self-esteem. In Dayton's words from
Rediscovering an Evangelical Heritage, "Discipline and a reordered lifestyle enable converts to rise in social class and
economic level, a process culminating in a middle-class
church like those against which the movement originally
protested. This new church is subtly transformed into a bas-
tion against those who would threaten its life, especially the
lower classes that were once a source of vitality."[17] The church

that once postured itself among the poor, on the wrong side of worldly power, has newfound worldly power, with wealth to protect, status to defend. It was from within these historical developments that Holiness evangelicals blurred the powers, found themselves defenders of the social status quo, lost their vision for women in ministry, and became complicit with racism and segregation. They moved from being on the right side of history to being on the wrong side as they moved from the right side of godly power to the wrong side of worldly power.

Liberation Theology: Being on the Right Side of Power

The notion of being on the wrong side of worldly power is not novel. For decades, liberation theologians have put forth the truth that God is recognized among the oppressed, on the wrong side of worldly power. God's power is released among the poor. It is among the powerless (in worldly terms), those with no access to worldly power, that we shall find God's power at work by His presence. This relation between power, posture, and discernment has been explored by Latin American, Feminist, Mujerista, Womanist, and Black liberation theologians. For them, the church has too often been on the side of worldly power when it needed instead to go and be with the oppressed in order to discern who God is and how His power is at work in the world.

Liberation theologians describe this dynamic as "the epistemological privilege" of the poor. God's "preferential option" is to work via His power among those who are open to Him. Mujerista theologian Ada María Isasi-Díaz says that we "can see and understand what the rich and privileged cannot. It is not that the poor and oppressed are morally superior or that they can see better. Their epistemological privilege is based on the fact that, because their point of view is not distorted by power and riches, they can see differently."[18] And so, deep within the wiring of liberation theology, a theological method emerges that teaches the church to discern what God is doing *not* by discerning the right side of history as seen from a privileged vantage point but rather by being present on the right side of godly power, postured among the powerless, where God is already at work.

In his groundbreaking book *God of the Oppressed*, Black liberation theologian James Cone explains that "to know Jesus is to know him as revealed in the struggle of the oppressed for freedom."[19] There is this searing illumination of God, "concrete signs of divine presence, among the lives of the poor." Cone describes this illumination as "the liberating power of black experience," where the relational power of God's presence is at work in the world, drawing people to reconciliation, justice, and renewal among the marginalized.[20]

Over and over again Cone talks about the problem of distance and "power over," the posture of White supremacy, which blinds even his own colleagues at Union Seminary from seeing and understanding God at work for justice in the world.[21] And so, Cone exemplifies the main theme of this book: if we want to discern what God is doing, if we desire to partake of God's power, we must resist being on the wrong side of worldly power, instead seeking the right side of godly power, under the power and presence of the Holy Spirit. Instead of trying to be on the right side of history, let us seek to be the church on the right side of God's power, participating in His work in the world.

Sexuality on the Right Side of Power

All this being said, the church seems prone to blurring the powers in order to accomplish God's justice. We are ever tempted to take the reins of top-down, coercive, legislative "power over" to get God's work done. How do we learn from the mistakes the White evangelical church has made as it has capitulated to the evils of slavery, patriarchy, and economic exploitation every time it has aligned itself with worldly power? How do we avoid making the same mistakes in relation to the social ills and conflicts that plague our cultures today? Will we work from the wrong side of power, aligning with power over, or will we make space for the power of God, the Holy Spirit, to work among us as we make space for God's presence to work in all the struggles we face. Can we be a different people?

The conflict over sexuality stands preeminent as one of those conflicts before us today. We are often warned against being on the wrong side of history regarding this conflict. As church leaders, we are tempted to issue a policy directive: our church "does not affirm" LGBTQ sexuality or our church "affirms" LGBTQ sexuality. But such edicts, in either direction, could miss the opportunity for God and His power to work among us. It may soothe the impatience, the hurt, the pain, or the insecurities among us. But it only works based on power and solves little of the bigger issues going on among us in the areas of sexuality and gender.

As already described, queer theorists teach us that within the dominant construals of male and female sexuality lie misogyny, coercion, sexualization of bodies, patriarchy, and toxicity in the guiding assumptions about what one must look like, act like, and feel like. Several theorists argue that lesbian or gay sexualities must escape the determinations of heterosexuality to truly be free from patriarchy, sexualization, and other maladies that plague human bodies in today's sexuality and gender cultures. To affirm or refuse to affirm LGBTQ sexuality with a policy does not address any of these issues. It does not address the ills within the heterosexual formations among us. It avoids discerning any pain among LGBTQ persons perpetuated by those heterosexual formations. Such policy statements in effect become bandages covering the antagonism, brokenness, and pain that simmers among us.

It could be that those among us who are gay, lesbian, bisexual, queer, or trans are calling into question a lot of the toxic sexuality and gender relations that have become hegemonic in our churches, unquestioned as natural, and endorsed as Christian and normative. The presence of LGBTQ persons among the church could be the moment to make space, listen, be convicted, be challenged, repent, and be transformed, all of us together, by what God by the power of the Holy Spirit might do among us. It therefore seems unwise to make policy statements as churches or denominations in these times of discernment. Let us instead offer a path of discipleship that is inclusive of all people—and heterosexuals should be first in line. Instead of seeking the right side of history, let us seek the way of God's power.

This may seem to fly in the face of those who see the church as once more on the wrong side of history in regard to sexuality. These folk see the church, just as with slavery, racism, women's rights, and economics, as being slow to affirm those who are marginalized. We must seize the levers of power to make things right. But again, as in all these other moments in church history, I urge the church to resist the ways of worldly power and instead be among those who identify as, or struggle with, LGBTQ sexualities. Let us make safe, welcoming, and inclusive spaces for conversation. Let us listen carefully, discerning and inviting the Holy Spirit to work among us.

In 2016, Andrew Marin conducted what is still the most extensive survey of LGBTQ persons ever done. Its participants spanned geography, age, and class in the United States. This largest-ever sampling (1,712 usable surveys) on record was overseen by authorities at Northwestern University and the

University of Chicago. The findings were stunning. Marin discovered that 86 percent of LGBTQ persons were from a church, and over three-quarters of these churched persons were from a conservative church. Most had attended church while growing up, and the majority had left church after they came out as LGBTQ.[22] When LGBTQ persons discussed why they left church, "theological difference over sin" was not the primary reason for leaving. Rather, it was the hate, disgust, coercion, the lack of safety, the lack of dialogue, the loss of trust in institutional authority.[23] They said things like, "I left church because I couldn't find one person who cared to listen to my story."[24]

One way to read this tragic litany of stories and statistics is that our LGBTQ brothers and sisters have suffered under the hegemonic structures of sexuality enforced by the churches via worldly power. In the process, the structure of this sexuality—and I am talking heterosexuality—has never been examined for its own toxicity, its cultural pollution, its enforcement of a "regime" that says you must look like this and feel like this to be a Christian.

In response, the easiest thing to do might be to enforce a corrective via worldly power—affirm LGBTQ as part of this enduring regime or in reaction to this regime—without ever examining, unwinding, questioning, and seeing what the Spirit is doing to disrupt and heal the entire sexual formation of the evangelical church. And so, as tempting as it is to use worldly power to enforce a viable solution—to affirm or not affirm—such an approach glosses over the smoldering cauldron that will erupt and destroy all of us eventually if we do not sit and listen, confess, repent, and let the Spirit move.

And so instead of using the wheel of worldly power, let all (heterosexuals go first) make space for the sweeping work of the Holy Spirit to convict and to lead us in lament, repentance, healing, reconciliation, and transformation. This is the way of godly power. Out of these spaces we shall discern the Spirit, allow Her to work, and unleash the forces of godly power among us. Let us be a truly different kind of people.

Can We Be a Different People, on the Right Side of Power?

We've seen God's power at work among the abolitionists, the feminist movements, and the wars on poverty through the church. We've also seen the church go cold toward justice on all these cultural sins when it aligns itself with worldly power. These stories teach us that the church is the church only when it sits on the right side of God's power. There God's power in Christ is unleashed among us by the Holy Spirit, and justice springs forth like a river, and people join the kingdom.

We've seen the church on the right side of power bring forth fruit again and again. We've seen how simple, humble communities, over a couple hundred years, rocked the Greco-Roman Empire in the first centuries of the early church.[25] In more recent days, we've seen how fifty or so prayer-meeting dinner fellowships in the 1950s South disrupted Jim Crow. Groups of three or four Black students met in this fashion at Woolworth diners across the South as organized by the Student Nonviolent Coordinating Committee (SNCC), and the civil rights movement was begun.[26] We've seen how localized Catholic base communities practicing the Eucharist together in Chile in the 1980s brought down the torture regime of the dictator Augusto Pinochet.[27] We've seen how individual lives, like those of Sister Félicité, Archbishop John Baptist Odama of Uganda, and their Christian communities lived among those hurting from the genocide and war of Rwanda and Uganda. Amid hatred and killing, they made space for God to work in conversations for peace and reconciliation, and thus they made space for goodness to take root. Resisting the worldly "power over" that was inculcated through colonialist rule, these Christians and their communities made space for godly power to work, and healing and transformation broke out.[28]

The list of such stories runs through the annals of Christian history. But they are often ignored or pushed aside by the more grandiose stories of immediate church success that comes with worldly power. But the church is the church only when it lives "under" the power of God. When the church lives this way, it is the church on the right side of power, not the "power over" of the world but the power of God put "to work in Christ when he raised him from the dead and seated him at his right hand in the heavenly places, far above all rule and authority and power and dominion, and above every name that is named, not only in this age but also in the age to come" (Eph. 1:20–21). It is this God we are called to serve. It is this church we are called to be. And in this faithfulness His kingdom shall be made real among us in all the places where we live, until "he has put all his enemies under his feet" (1 Cor. 15:25), and He shall reign forever and ever.

ACKNOWLEDGMENTS

I cannot recall when I started to think seriously about questions of power. I know the problem of power has been on my mind since the days of my youth as a pastor's kid in elementary school. I remember watching my father lead and engage conflict with a marvelous humility, which left an indelible mark on my thinking about power. In seminary, I wrote my master's thesis in New Testament on power, authority, and gifts in the New Testament church. I was relentless in uncovering what the New Testament revealed about power. When I left the church for a bit in my twenties and took up a job in the financial services industry, I witnessed the abuse of power like nowhere else I'd ever seen. Sadly, as I reentered the church in my early thirties, I saw similar problems in the church and the leadership summits of that time. Truth be told, since high school I have been obsessed with the problem of power and how it works itself out in culture, politics, and specifically the church of Jesus Christ. This book is the fruition of that journey.

And so it's hard to know where to begin in acknowledging everyone who has impacted this project on power. But there are some obvious dues to be acknowledged. First, thank you to my graduate students at Northern Seminary who have studied with me. Our conversations on power, the pushbacks to my class lectures, the times we've sat around with a brew, all have contributed to this book. Thanks to friends who read the early versions of the manuscript and gave me verbal feedback. Thanks to the pastor groups who I presented to and who asked good questions and probed places that needed clarification. Thanks to people like Gino Curcuruto, David Boshart, and Daniel Hutton, who read the early manuscript and gave good feedback. Thanks to Don Dayton, who met with me before his death and talked through many of the concepts in this book, some of them working off his own work. My Northern colleague Scot McKnight helped me more than a few times on my exegesis inquiries. None of these people necessarily agreed with everything I wrote. Their critical engagements were helpful. Thanks to Keith Matthews and Don Thorsen, who invited me to present the 2020 Robertson Holiness Lectures at Azusa Pacific University. It was there that I fleshed out the beginnings of the ideas that drive this book. There are many more people to thank. My life is full of generous encouragers to my work.

Northern Seminary of Chicago, where I am a professor, has been of great support to my life and ministry. We've been through an enormous struggle these past few years, and I commend our current leadership for leading us through the conflicts for righteousness, justice, and God's power at work among us to bring healing and an embodiment of God's mission for the world. The staff of Northern Seminary has been amazing as they have borne the weight and the pain of some bad stuff we had to work out in the way the seminary was being run. The lessons of this book couldn't be more timely for us as we continue to move deeper into the mission of Northern Seminary for this time and this place in our history. Several members of the current staff, and some who no longer work at Northern, have been heroes during this time. I pray they will be blessed and see the fruits of their labors in the days to come. I dedicate this book to them because they have been a stunning reminder to me of how important it is that God's people, in the service of God's mission, be on the side of God's power for His work to be done and empowered.

Special thanks to Eric Salo, my editor, and Erin Smith, who supervised the marketing (I love the cover of this book), as well as Bob Hosack, executive editor, who guided this book through publication, all of whom make Baker Publishing and Brazos Press a great place to work with in publishing a book.

Last, many thanks to Rae Ann, to whom I am husband, and Max, to whom I am dad, for all the times I asked them to be quiet in the house (especially during COVID) so I could concentrate on writing and researching this book. Their forbearance, support, and general all-around presence in my life make this book and a lot of other things possible. They give me added motivation to pursue God's faithfulness in our times.

NOTES

Introduction

1. Stanley Hauerwas (among others) has criticized the modern presumption of democratic liberalism that maintains the distinction between the spheres of religion and politics by sequestering religious/Christian convictions to the private lives of individuals while leaving the work of justice to the public rules of politics. Christians are therefore left to the government to work for justice under the rules of the state as their only option. In a similar vein, my project in this book extends this critique and refuses to restrict God's power to the private and personal lives of individuals, thereby leaving the public work of justice to the coercive power of the state and the public. I continue to see the church, by its presence in the social realities we live in, making space for the transforming power of God to disrupt oppressive systems and bring healing in the world in which we live and its cultures of injustice. This critique of democracy and political liberalism runs throughout Hauerwas's oeuvre. See, e.g., Hauerwas, *Community of Character* (Notre Dame, IN: University of Notre Dame Press, 1981), chap. 4; Hauerwas, *Wilderness Wanderings* (Boulder, CO: Westview, 1997), chap. 3.

2. Jemar Tisby, *The Color of Compromise: The Truth about the American Church's Complicity with Racism* (Grand Rapids: Zondervan, 2019).

3. Anthea Butler, *White Evangelical Racism: The Politics of Morality in America* (Chapel Hill: University of North Carolina Press, 2021).

4. Kristin Kobes Du Mez, *Jesus and John Wayne: How White Evangelicals Corrupted a Faith and Fractured a Nation* (New York: Liveright, 2021).

5. Kevin M. Kruse, *One Nation under God: How Corporate America Invented Christian America* (New York: Basic Books, 2015); John Fea, *Believe Me: The Evangelical Road to Donald Trump* (Grand Rapids: Eerdmans, 2018).

Chapter 1 Defining Power

1. This account is fictional, drawing on personal experiences as well as Elijah Drake's depiction of visiting a similar church in Michigan. Elijah Drake, "Visiting the Local MAGA Church," January 2, 2022, https://www.elijahdrake.com/churchexperience/localchurch.

2. Max Weber, *Economy and Society* (Berkeley: University of California Press, 1978), 53. For a concise tracing of how the field of sociology and its main figures built on Weber's conceptualization, see Isidor Wallimann, Nicholas Ch. Tatsis, and George V. Zito, "On Max Weber's Definition of Power," *Australian and New Zealand Journal of Sociology* 13 (1977): 231–35.

3. Robert A. Dahl, "The Concept of Power," *Behavioral Science* 2 (1957): 202–3.

4. Friedrich Nietzsche, *The Will to Power*, trans. Walter Kaufmann and R. J. Hollingdale (New York: Vintage, 1968).

5. Michel Foucault, *Power/Knowledge: Selected Interviews and Other Writings, 1972–1977*, trans. and ed. Colin Gordon (New York: Vintage, 1980), 94. Louis Althusser calls this process "interpellation." When an authority such as a police officer hails a person on the street, and that person turns around and recognizes themself in the address, they are now a "subject" whose self-understanding is determined by the power at work in policing. See Louis Althusser, "Ideology and Ideological State Apparatuses," in *Lenin and Philosophy, and Other Essays*, trans. Ben Brewster (London: New Left Books, 1977), 163. The French sociologist Pierre Bourdieu covers similar territory in his concept "symbolic power." He contends that there are modes of cultural domination that are maintained over subjects through everyday social habits. It is power wielded in ways that are tacit, the subject being unaware. Within these modes of power, as seen in education or systems of economics, the individual is put in their place within the social hierarchies. According to Bourdieu, this form of soft power

makes possible discriminatory and even injurious effects, including patriarchy and racism, without the subject recognizing it. Bourdieu, *Language and Symbolic Power*, ed. John B. Thompson, trans. Gino Raymond and Matthew Adamson (Cambridge: Polity, 1992).

6. Foucault called these practices "disciplinary procedures." Foucault, *Discipline and Punish: The Birth of the Prison*, trans. Alan Sheridan (New York: Vintage, 1991), 155–230.

7. This process of one's identity being formed by the power one submits to was called "subjection" by Judith Butler: "But if, following Foucault, we understand power as *forming* the subject as well, as providing the very condition of its existence and the trajectory of its desire, then power is not simply what we oppose, but also . . . what we depend upon for our existence and what we harbor and preserve in the beings that we are. . . . Subjection consists precisely in this fundamental dependency on a discourse we never chose but that, paradoxically, initiates and sustains our agency." Butler, *The Psychic Life of Power: Theories in Subjection* (Stanford, CA: Stanford University Press, 1997), 2.

0. Foucault defined these workings as "biopower."

9. This is the argument first carried out by Karl Marx, and then in more complex and various ways via the critique of ideology. Jonathan Tran, working with critical theory, exposes the way racism is an ideological justification of economic exploitation of various ethnic groups in the history of the United States. Tran, *Asian Americans and the Spirit of Racial Capitalism* (Oxford: Oxford University Press, 2021).

10. "Gaze" is a significant concept for Foucault. How we are seen illumines so much as to how we see ourselves and submit to various regimes of knowledge and power (e.g., medical gaze, male gaze).

11. The women's suffrage movement, working for the right of women to vote, began before the Civil War but led to the Nineteenth Amendment, giving women the right to vote in 1920. The initial focus for this feminist movement was the same right for women to vote as was possessed by men. This movement therefore tended to frame power in terms of equal individual rights. The focus on individual empowerment was not original or new to this movement. It was grounded in the Enlightenment. For example, a key Enlightenment figure in the grounding of power in the individual is Thomas Hobbes. In *Leviathan* he describes an individual person's natural

(or original) power in terms of given innate skills, which are faculties that enable a person to do something, and instrumental power, which can be acquired to enable a person to achieve even more of something. This provides a foundation for Hobbes's contention that each person's abilities can be united with the abilities of others in a commonwealth to accomplish even more as a communal aspiration. See Hobbes, *Leviathan*, ed. Marshall Missner (New York: Routledge, 2008), 54–56.

12. Womanist political theorist Patricia Hill Collins says, "Black women have not conceptualized our quest for empowerment as one of replacing white male authorities with ourselves as benevolent Black female ones. Instead, African American women have overtly rejected theories of power based on domination in order to embrace an alternative vision of power based on a humanist vision of self actualization, self definition and self determination." Collins, *Black Feminist Thought: Knowledge, Consciousness, and the Politics of Empowerment* (New York: Routledge, 1991), 111. Amy Allen, of Penn State University, argues for a nuanced understanding of power as empowerment and agency in her review of Iris Marion Young's *Justice and the Politics of Difference* (Princeton: Princeton University Press, 1990), in Allen, "Power and the Politics of Difference: Oppression, Empowerment, and Transnational Justice," *Hypatia* 23, no. 3 (2008): 156–72. For another take on this, see J. Ann Tickner, "Hans Morgenthau's Principles of Political Realism: A Feminist Reformulation," *Millennium—Journal of International Studies* 17, no. 3 (1988): 429–40.

13. For a womanist take on this, see bell hooks, *Ain't I a Woman? Black Women and Feminism* (Boston: South End, 1981); Collins, *Black Feminist Thought*; and Audre Lorde, "Uses of the Erotic: The Erotic as Power," in *Audre Lorde's Sister Outsider: Essays and Speeches* (Trumansburg, NY: Crossing Press, 1984), 5.

14. For instance, see Susan Moller Okin, *Justice, Gender, and the Family* (New York: Basic Books, 1989). The backdrop to this movement was the influential distributive account of power as framed by political theorist William E. Connolly. See Connolly, *The Terms of Political Discourse*, 3rd ed. (Princeton: Princeton University Press, 1993), esp. chap. 3.

15. See Iris Marion Young, "Throwing like a Girl: A Phenomenology of Feminine Body Comportment, Motility and Spatiality," *Human Studies* 3, no. 2 (1980): 137–56. Young is a premier example of this

thinking. She argues for new and inventive ways of using phenomenology to think through the bodies and social constructs of being
a woman in society.

16. Amy Allen, for instance, argues convincingly that personal and
collective empowerment has a place as a mode of power within Iris
Marion Young's understanding of power. Allen, "Power and the Politics of Difference." Likewise, Judith Butler makes a case for resistance
from within the construct. Since gender is not something one is, but
something one does, a culturally sanctioned doing of gender, then the
way of undoing it lies in the cultural means by which it is produced.
In Butler's words, we can only rethink the "possibilities for sexuality
and identity within the terms of power itself." Butler, *Gender Trouble:
Feminism and the Subversion of Identity* (New York: Routledge, 1990),
30. See Anita Brady and Tony Schirato, *Understanding Judith Butler*
(Los Angeles: Sage, 2011), 43–50.

17. Butler, a leading voice of third-wave feminism and queer theory
from the 1990s, sees power as so woven into the gender and/or sexuality constructs of culture that there is no possibility for the distribution of power apart from disrupting the constructs themselves. In
Butler's words, "If sexuality is culturally constructed within existing
power relations, then the postulation of a normative sexuality that is
'before,' 'outside,' or 'beyond' power is a cultural impossibility and a
politically impracticable dream, one that postpones the concrete and
contemporary task of rethinking subversive possibilities for sexuality and identity within the terms of power itself." Butler, *Gender
Trouble*, 30.

18. Young, *Justice and the Politics of Difference*, chap. 1, esp. 30–34.

19. The provincial government of Newfoundland/Labrador (Can-
ada) has issued a concise worksheet on nine types of violence and
abuse that it seeks to prevent in its legal and social services. It is an
excellent concise summary of types of violence. The nine types are
physical violence, sexual violence, emotional violence, psychological
violence, spiritual violence, cultural violence, verbal abuse, financial
abuse, and neglect. "Nine Types of Violence and Abuse," Newfound-
land/Labrador, 2014, https://www.gov.nl.ca/vpi/files/nine_types_of
_violence.pdf.

20. Slavoj Žižek, *Violence: Six Sideways Reflections* (New York:
Picador, 2008), 9–15. Because poverty is a constant, systematic form
of violence, sudden violent incidents will attract more notice.

21. Walter Benjamin's *Toward a Critique of Violence* was foundational for raising a whole new awareness of the violence at the heart of a functioning society's laws and economy. He named "mythical violence" as that which legitimates a society's laws, and he gave the name "divine violence" to that which disrupts mythical violence, leading to revolutions. Benjamin, *Toward a Critique of Violence* (Stanford, CA: Stanford University Press, 2021).

22. For these themes in King, see his speech "The Power of Nonviolence," address at the University of California at Berkeley, 1957, in *A Testament of Hope: The Essential Writings and Speeches of Martin Luther King Jr.*, ed. James M. Washington (San Francisco: Harper-SanFrancisco, 1991), 12–15 and 334–37.

23. Butler, *The Force of Nonviolence: An Ethico-Political Bind* (New York: Verso, 2020), 40–50.

24. Butler, *Force of Nonviolence*, 21–24.

25. Cornel West and George Yancy, "Power Is Everywhere, but Love Is Supreme," *New York Times*, May 29, 2019, https://www.nytimes.com/2019/05/29/opinion/cornel-west-power-love.html.

26. Mahatma Gandhi, *Selected Political Writings*, ed. Dennis Dalton (Indianapolis: Hackett, 1996), 29. Ghandi discusses how anger often undercuts this *Satyagraha*. Anger, when a form of reaction that lashes out in violence, disrupts and counteracts this power.

27. For a summary of these concepts, see Gustavo Gutiérrez, *Essential Writings*, ed. James B. Nickoloff (Maryknoll, NY: Orbis Books, 1996), chap. 2.

28. Mujerista theologian Ada María Isasi-Díaz says that the marginalized "can see and understand what the rich and privileged cannot. It is not that the poor and oppressed are morally superior or that they can see better. Their epistemological privilege is based on the fact that, because their point of view is not distorted by power and riches, they can see differently." Ada Maria Isasi-Díaz, "Mujeristas: A Name of Our Own," *Christian Century*, May 24–31, 1989, 560.

29. Sarah Schulman, *Conflict Is Not Abuse: Overstating Harm, Community Responsibility, and the Duty of Repair* (Vancouver: Arsenal Pulp Press, 2016), 57–60.

30. For one of the better descriptions of how the base communities of Chile resisted the torture of the Pinochet regime, see William T. Cavanaugh, *Torture and Eucharist: Theology, Politics, and the Body of Christ* (Oxford: Blackwell, 1998).

31. Jürgen Moltmann, a supporter and contributor to the liberation theology movement, is an example of one who blends "power with" with "power over," arguing, in essence, that Christians can discern and know God's will and participate in violent revolution in the name of liberation. Arne Rasmussen narrates the progression in Moltmann's thought in regard to pacifism, violence, and revolution in Rasmussen, *The Church as Polis: From Political Theology to Theological Politics as Exemplified by Jürgen Moltmann and Stanley Hauerwas* (Notre Dame, IN: University of Notre Dame Press, 1995), chap. 7.

32. Joseph Ratzinger, "Instruction on Certain Aspects of the 'Theology of Liberation,'" in *Christianity and Modern Politics*, ed. Louisa S. Hulett (Berlin: de Gruyter, 1993), 422–35, also available at https://www.vatican.va/roman_curia/congregations/cfaith/documents/rc_con_cfaith_doc_19840806_theology-liberation_en.html.

33. As quoted in E. J. Dionne Jr., "Bishop Assails Liberation Theology," *New York Times*, December 1, 1985.

34. Anabaptist theologian John Howard Yoder warned of this proclivity in liberation theology and its Roman Catholic movements. Yoder, *The War of the Lamb: The Ethics of Nonviolence and Peacemaking*, ed. Glen Harold Stassen, Mark Thiessen Nation, and Matt Hamsher (Grand Rapids: Brazos, 2009), 171–72.

In citing Yoder, we must not forget the history of his sexual abuse against his students in the later years of his academic career, and we must discern this while reading his work. I will refrain from citing Yoder in the main text of this book out of respect for Yoder's victims. Nonetheless, I do cite Yoder in the notes where he has had influence on the ideas herein. I do this with discernment, watching for the areas of his work blighted by the abuse he carried out against his female students. I believe this is a better option than to not cite him at all and in essence cover up his influence, which remains pervasive in the peace tradition out of which I am working. Such an approach, I suggest, makes possible further discernment of whether and how Yoder should be read.

35. See James Cone, *The Cross and the Lynching Tree* (Maryknoll, NY: Orbis Books, 2011), 8, 9. Cone also describes the issues of patriarchy and misogyny, sure evidence of "power over" that arose from time to time among the movement versus postures of nonviolence. For the problem of sexism and patriarchy within the early Black theology

movement, see James Cone, *Martin & Malcom & America: A Dream or a Nightmare* (Maryknoll, NY: Orbis Books, 1991), chap. 10 ("Nothing but Men"); Cone, *Black Theology and Black Power* (Maryknoll, NY: Orbis Books, 1989), x–xi.

36. For a complete account of these developments and more within the SNCC movement, see Charles Marsh, *The Beloved Community: How Faith Shapes Social Justice, from the Civil Rights Movement to Today* (New York: Basic Books, 2005), 112–20, and esp. chap. 6 ("Unfinished Business"). In regard to the reappearance of Jim Crow, see Michelle Alexander's *The New Jim Crow: Mass Incarceration in the Age of Colorblindness* (New York: New Press, 2010), which shows historically how racism took other systemic forms in the culture, especially in the legal and incarceration systems, and needed new social engagements from outside the government if they were to be exposed and engaged for social change.

37. This is the thesis of Marsh, *Beloved Community*.

38. Robert K. Greenleaf, *The Power of Servant-Leadership: Essays*, ed. Larry C. Spears (San Francisco: Berrett-Koehler, 1998); Greenleaf, *Servant Leadership: A Journey into the Nature of Legitimate Power and Greatness*, ed. Larry C. Spears (New York: Paulist Press, 1977). For further exploration of how servant leadership defaults to a technique for using power over, see Christena Cleveland, "The Hole in Our Servant Leadership," *Christianity Today*, October 26, 2015, https://www.christianitytoday.com/ct/2015/november/hole-in-our-servant-leadership.html; David Fitch, *The Great Giveaway: Reclaiming the Mission of the Church from Big Business, Parachurch Organizations, Psychotherapy, Consumer Capitalism, and Other Modern Maladies* (Grand Rapids: Baker Books, 2005), chap. 3.

39. For a general review of the status of servant leadership and an evaluation of whether the term "servant leadership" is an oxymoron, see Jim Heskett, "Why Isn't 'Servant Leadership' More Prevalent?," *Harvard Business School*, May 1, 2013, https://hbswk.hbs.edu/item/why-isnt-servant-leadership-more-prevalent.

40. French philosopher and social theorist Jacques Ellul makes a version of this case in his *The Technological Society*. For him, "technique" refers to more than the tools we pursue to take control of outcomes in every field of human activity. "Technique" is part of a sociology that engulfs us, with values, approaches to life, and a constant seeking of efficiency that subordinates all parts of human life

to its power. Ellul, often accused of being dismissive in his assessment, is pointing to this overwhelming tendency in Westernized culture to default to means that give us "power over" people; in the process, he maintains, we give up what it means to be truly human. Ellul, *The Technological Society*, trans. John Wilkinson (New York: Vintage, 1964).

41. Martin Luther King Jr.'s approach to nonviolence could be read as a tactic to coerce certain outcomes, as a tactic of "power over." See the work of historian David Chappell, "The Radicalism of Martin Luther King Jr.'s Nonviolent Resistance: His Most Brilliant Innovation Was a Tactic That Managed to Be Forceful—and Nonviolent," *Washington Post*, January 15, 2018, https://www.washingtonpost.com /news/made-by-history/wp/2018/01/15/the-radicalism-of-martin -luther-kings-nonviolent-resistance.

42. I'm influenced here by Stanley Hauerwas's argument (via John Howard Yoder) that differentiates functional pacifism from christological pacifism. For Hauerwas's christological pacifism, we choose the way and practice of nonviolence not because it will function as a tactic to achieve a predetermined outcome (e.g., the end of war) but because Jesus is Lord and He has called us to give up control of the world and live under His power, wherever He is taking the world. This theme runs through much of Hauerwas's work. See, e.g., Hauerwas, *Performing the Faith: Bonhoeffer and the Practice of Nonviolence* (Grand Rapids: Brazos, 2004), chap. 7. See also an exposition of christological pacifism in Tripp York and Justin Bronson Barringer, eds., *A Faith Not Worth Fighting For* (Eugene, OR: Cascade Books, 2012).

Chapter 2 Worldly Power and God's Power

1. I believe a case can be made that the power Paul describes in Eph. 3:20 Paul is locating as being "among us" versus just "in us." I follow the International Standard Version translation in this regard.

2. Craig Van Gelder and Dwight Zscheile examine the issue of human agency in the work of God in their *The Missional Church in Perspective: Mapping Trends and Shaping the Conversation* (Grand Rapids: Baker Academic, 2011). They assert that discipleship for the church in mission must move from a focus on the imitation of Christ to participation in Christ (119). The stress on human agency in imitation models puts the focus on human performance. This does not account for human sin. Instead, that agency must come under

participation in the work of the Trinity in the world. This is made possible by a renewal of the discernment of the work of the Spirit (110–11). This point I see as running parallel to the point I'm making here.

3. Stanley Hauerwas, *The Peaceable Kingdom* (Notre Dame, IN: University of Notre Dame Press, 1983), 104.

4. This way of nuancing godly power with the preposition "under" I owe to a discussion at the Jesus Collective UNITE 22 conference in Oakville, Ontario. There my friends pushed me to define "godly power" as "power for." I did not resonate with the directional nature of that preposition, and I believe we settled on "under."

5. Note that a large part of Mark 10, leading up to vv. 42–45, pictures Jesus as undercutting worldly "power over." From undercutting patriarchy in the old ways of divorce, where a man can leave his wife but she cannot leave her husband (vv. 2–12), to the way we approach children from an "over" perspective (vv. 13–16), to the rich man being told to sell all he has and give the money to the poor (v. 21), Jesus is undercutting various forms of worldly power.

6. Richard A. Horsley reads Jesus's works of healings and exorcisms in these terms. See *Jesus and Empire: The Kingdom of God and the New World Disorder* (Minneapolis: Fortress, 2002).

7. N. T. Wright, for instance, seeks to make this clear in his *John for Everyone: Part 2, Chapters 11–21*, 2nd ed. (Louisville: Westminster John Knox, 2004), 114–15: "Jesus' answer is both apparently incriminating and deeply revealing. His kingdom (yes, he agrees he has a kingdom; Pilate seizes on this) doesn't come from this world. Please note, he doesn't say, as some translations have put it, 'my kingdom is not *of* this world'; that would imply that his 'kingdom' was altogether other-worldly, a spiritual or heavenly reality that had nothing to do with the present world at all. That is not the point. Jesus, after all, taught his disciples to pray that God's kingdom would come 'on earth as in heaven.'"

8. I am drawing heavily in these paragraphs from Theodore Hiebert, "Rethinking Dominion Theology," *Direction Journal* 24, no. 2 (Fall 1996): 16–25; Hiebert, *The Yahwist's Landscape: Nature and Religion in Early Israel* (Minneapolis: Fortress, 2008), chaps. 1–2. Stanley Hauerwas critiques John Paul II's interpretation of these Genesis passages in terms of humans being cocreators with God and "domination." Hauerwas refers to Gerhard von Rad's work to

substantiate that humans, as created in the image of God, are God's representatives, not partners in creation. They reflect God's creation and maintain what has already been completed. "Subdue" and "dominion" should therefore not be interpreted in terms of those who rule over but as those who maintain and cultivate God's good order in creation in cooperation with and submission to God. For Hauerwas's entire treatment of John Paul II's treatment of Gen. 1, see Hauerwas, *In Good Company: The Church as Polis* (Notre Dame, IN: University of Notre Dame Press, 1995), 111–14.

9. A good summary of these many theories, written in popular prose, can be found in Brian Klaas, *Corruptible: Who Gets Power and How It Changes Us* (New York: Scribner, 2021), 17–36.

10. G. K. Beale argues that the Genesis account of the garden of Eden portrays Eden as the first sanctuary, a recapitulation of the first temple. Beale, *The Temple and the Church's Mission: A Biblical Theology of the Dwelling Place of God* (Downers Grove, IL: InterVarsity, 2004), 66–80. See also Jon D. Levenson, *Sinai and Zion: An Entry into the Jewish Bible* (New York: HarperOne, 1987).

11. I am drawing almost entirely upon John Nugent's exposition of the monarchy in Israel in Nugent, *The Politics of Yahweh: John Howard Yoder, the Old Testament, and the People of God* (Eugene, OR: Cascade Books, 2011), chap. 4.

12. Nugent, *Politics of Yahweh*, 49–50. That it was God's way to govern Israel with a plurality of leaders in mutal relation is supported by the "Let us" of Gen. 1:26. Ingrid Faro reiterates the argument that the "us" of 1:26 is God addressing the "divine council." This divine council, an assembly of spiritual beings, is the way God shares power in governing the universe. Unwilling to coerce through "power over," God governs jointly. See Faro, *Demystifying Evil: A Biblical and Personal Exploration* (Downers Grove, IL: InterVarsity, 2023), chap. 12.

13. Instead of conflicts and territorial issues being navigated via the miracles of God, Israel turned to violence. John H. Yoder, according to John Nugent, suggested that "not only did they assimilate non-Israelite groups to hew their wood and draw their water, they also adopted non-Israelite leaders to run their wars." Nugent, *Politics of Yahweh*, 61.

14. These paragraphs have been influenced by Gregory Boyd, *The Crucifixion of the Warrior God: Interpreting the Old Testament's Violent Portraits of God in Light of the Cross*, 2 vols. (Minneapolis:

Fortress, 2017); William Webb and Gordon Oeste, *Bloody, Brutal and Barbaric? Wrestling with Troubling War Texts* (Downers Grove, IL: IVP Academic, 2109); and Webb's thesis that there is a redemptive historical movement of God within Scripture. God enters history on its terms, choosing to work through godly power, not worldly power, incrementally over time through relational covenantal obedience of a people. Through this entire treatment of Scripture I am also heavily indebted to Nugent, *Politics of Yahweh*.

15. Boyd, *Crucifixion*, 2:963.

16. Boyd, *Crucifixion*, 2:975–76.

17. Boyd, *Crucifixion*, 2:989–91. Boyd relies heavily on Walter Brueggemann, *Divine Presence amid Violence: Contextualizing the Book of Joshua* (Eugene, OR: Cascade Books, 2009), 15–44.

18. Much of this account of the "servant songs" draws on John Nugent's account of Yoder's reading of them. Nugent, *Politics of Yahweh*, 69–73.

19. Timothy G. Gombis, *Power in Weakness: Paul's Transformed Vision for Ministry* (Grand Rapids: Eerdmans, 2021), 145–47.

20. Kathy Ehrensberger argues that those who challenged Paul's understanding of apostleship in 2 Corinthians were most likely shaped according to the Hellenistic and Roman cultural milieu of the day. In this milieu, leadership was constrained to the wise, wellborn, and powerful. You had to be a person of good standing, honor, rhetorical eloquence. Most of all, she says, you did not perform manual labor but benefited from the work of others. These privileges were reserved for the few. The structure of Roman society was a static hierarchy "where establishing oneself in positions of status was a constant competition for positions of domination and subordination." Leaders are thus men who prove they are competitive, strong enough to dominate and keep others in their place. Ehrensberger says that those who challenged Paul's apostolic authority were thinking of leadership in these terms. Paul did not live up to these terms, acknowledged that he did not, and furthermore, refused to grasp for leadership on these terms of "power over." Ehrensberger, *Paul and the Dynamics of Power: Communication and Interaction in the Early Christ-Movement* (London: T&T Clark, 2009), 103.

21. Michael Gorman, "Although/Because He Was in the Form of God: The Theological Significance of Paul's Master Story (Phil 2:6–11)," *Journal of Theological Interpretation* 1, no. 2 (2007): 147–69.

22. These are just a few of the scholars who have influenced this interpretation of Revelation. Key texts include Michael J. Gorman, *Reading Revelation Responsibly: Uncivil Worship and Witness; Following the Lamb into a New Creation* (Eugene, OR: Cascade Books, 2011); Loren L. Johns, *The Lamb Christology of the Apocalypse: An Investigation into Its Origins and Rhetorical Force* (Eugene, OR: Wipf & Stock, 2014); Richard Bauckham, *The Theology of the Book of Revelation* (Cambridge: Cambridge University Press, 1993).

23. "The shock of this reversal discloses the central mystery of the Apocalypse: God overcomes the world not through a show of force but through the suffering and death of Jesus, 'the faithful witness' (1:5)." Richard B. Hays, *The Moral Vision of the New Testament: Community, Cross, New Creation; A Contemporary Introduction to New Testament Ethics* (San Francisco: HarperSanFrancisco, 1996), 174, quoted in Gorman, *Reading Revelation Responsibly*, 108.

24. John R. Yeatts, *Revelation* (Scottdale, PA: Herald, 2003), 27.

25. Gorman, *Reading Revelation Responsibly*, 154–55.

26. J. Denny Weaver says, "The supposed battle scenes are not really battles at all." Weaver, *The Nonviolent Atonement* (Grand Rapids: Eerdmans, 2001), 32.

27. Gorman, *Reading Revelation Responsibly*, 155.

28. The sociologist scholar of power Steven Lukes outlines the history of the two terms within the fields of sociology in Lukes, "Power and Authority," in *A History of Sociological Analysis*, ed. Tom Bottomore and Robert Nisbet (London: Heinemann, 1979), 638–39. Bengt Holmberg pioneered the use of sociology in the study of the New Testament. For his description of how "power" versus "authority" has been used in the history of sociology, see Holmberg, *Paul and Power: The Structure of Authority in the Primitive Church as Reflected in the Pauline Epistles* (Minneapolis: Fortress, 1980), 125–35.

29. A full reading of the entries in Bauer's lexicon gives nuance to this description. Walter Bauer, William F. Arndt, F. Wilbur Gingrich, and Frederick W. Danker, *A Greek-English Lexicon of the New Testament and Other Early Christian Literature*, 2nd ed. (Chicago: University of Chicago Press, 1979), 207–8, 277–79. Likewise, Walter Wink exposits these two terms with all the nuances of the Jewish world prior to and concurrent with the New Testament. I am summarizing this research as it applies to the issues of worldly power versus godly power. See Wink, *Naming the Powers: The Language of Power*

in the New Testament (Philadelphia: Fortress, 1984), 15–17, 157–63. Stephen Sykes gives a helpful etymology on how the two words have been translated into English versions of the Bible. Sykes, *Power and Christian Theology* (London: Continuum, 2006), 3–4.

30. This notion of power at work in the life of Jesus and the differentiation between *dynamis* and *exousia* in the Gospels is drawn from Gerald Hawthorne, *The Presence and the Power* (Dallas: Word, 1991), 154–60.

31. These definitions of *dynamis* as God's active power released via the *exousia* (authority) of God in Christ as used in the Gospels is painstakingly charted in C. K. Barrett, *The Holy Spirit and the Gospel Tradition* (London: SPCK, 1947), chap. 5. *Exousia* is the authority antecedent to *dynamis*, the release of divine active power (79).

32. Again, there will be times when power is used to implement preventive measures that preserve people's lives. Here using legal power and "power over" can make sense. And we Christians should give aid and support to these governmental means. But in the church, Paul says we do not use even "legal" measures, lawsuits, to work out our life together (1 Cor. 6:1–8). Elsewhere, the use of "power over" must never become the "go to" means to engage our lives and our world for God. For God has work to do beyond merely preserving our society.

Chapter 3 The Persistent Temptation to Blur the Powers

1. All of these quotes and events are documented in Mike Cosper, "State of Emergency," episode 7 of *The Rise and Fall of Mars Hill* (podcast), August 9, 2021, produced by *Christianity Today*, https://www .christianitytoday.com/ct/podcasts/rise-and-fall-of-mars-hill/mars -hill-mark-driscoll-podcast-state-of-emergency.html.

2. A full account of these events written by Jonna Petry, wife of elder Paul Petry, is available at "My Story," Joyful Exiles, March 19, 2012, https://joyfulexiles.com/2012/03/19/my-story-by-jonna-petry.

3. I draw this phrase from one of the defining histories of the early church that draws out its nonviolent, noncoercive life and ministry in the world: Alan Kreider, *The Patient Ferment of the Early Church: The Improbable Rise of Christianity in the Roman Empire* (Grand Rapids: Baker Academic, 2016).

4. Justin Martyr, *First Apology* 39, in *Patrologia Graeca*, ed. Jacques-Paul Migne, 162 vols. (Paris, 1857–86), 6:39. Perhaps even

more stunning is that Justin Martyr appears to be talking about the first Christian conversions from the Roman military. See Kirk R. MacGregor, "Nonviolence in the Early Church and Christian Obedience," *Themelios* 33, no. 1 (2008): 17.

5. Kreider, *Patient Ferment*, 210.

6. John Howard Yoder says, "Were Christians before Constantine pacifists? Certainly not, if we give the term an ahistorically modern definition. . . . Yet none of the ways in which they were not modern pacifists allows us to say that they were non-pacifists or anti-pacifists." Yoder, "War as a Moral Problem in the Early Church: The Historian's Hermeneutical Assumptions," in *The Pacifist Impulse in Historical Perspective*, ed. Harvey L. Dyck (Toronto: University of Toronto Press, 1996), 102.

7. Peter J. Leithart acknowledges the anecdotal evidence of the rejection of violence and military service among the early church communities but suggests that the evidence is still "small, divided and ambiguous." Leithart, *Defending Constantine: The Twilight of an Empire and the Dawn of Christendom* (Downers Grove, IL: IVP Academic, 2010), 278.

8. For evidence friendly toward seeing the early church as nonviolent in its practice of living, see John Howard Yoder, *Christian Attitudes to War, Peace, and Revolution* (Grand Rapids: Brazos, 2009), chap. 3; Michael G. Long, ed., *Christian Peace and Nonviolence: A Documentary History* (Maryknoll, NY: Orbis Books, 2011); Ronald J. Sider, *The Early Church on Killing: A Comprehensive Sourcebook on War, Abortion, and Capital Punishment* (Grand Rapids: Baker Academic, 2012). For a critical look at this literature, see Leithart, *Defending Constantine*, chap. 12. Jennifer Otto not only critiques this literature; she asks whether it matters if the early church was nonviolent. See Otto, "Were the Early Christians Pacifists? Does It Matter?," *Conrad Grebel Review* 35, no. 3 (Fall 2017): 267–79.

9. Kreider, *Patient Ferment*, 107, and chap. 5 ("Communities as Cultures of Patience").

10. With conciseness and yet great nuance, Stephen Sykes describes this transformation in Eusebius and succeeding generations in "The Affirmation of Power," in *Power and Christian Theology* (London: Continuum, 2006), 27–53.

11. The "fall of the church" narrative describes the fateful turn of the alignment of church with state power that happened in Constantinian

Rome, which led to its corruption. This narrative is not peculiar to the Anabaptist, Radical Reformation tradition alone. Figures as wide-ranging as Francis of Assisi, John Wycliffe, Jan Hus, Bernard of Clairvaux, and Dante all employed the "fall of the church" narrative in some way. See Daniel H. Williams, "Constantine, Nicaea and the 'Fall of the Church,'" in *Christian Origins: Theology, Rhetoric and Community*, ed. Lewis Ayres and S. Gareth Jones (London: Routledge, 1998), 117–20. Yves Congar has a different account of the same blurring of powers from a Catholic perspective. He sees the time around Pope Gregory VIII, late in the twelfth century, when the church reconnected with the Roman Empire, as the time when the clergy separated themselves from the laity and took on legal institutional authority. Congar sees hierarchy as within and under the posture of service to the living Christ. Unfortunately, as Congar sees it, beginning with Gregory VIII, and then accelerating after the Council of Trent, ecclesiology turned increasingly to upholding and defending the hierarchy of the institution. See Congar, *Power and Poverty in the Church*, trans. Jennifer Nicholson (London: Chapman, 1964). Congar, deeply involved in the councils of Vatican II, remained disgruntled with regard to this issue. See Congar, "Moving towards a Pilgrim Church," in *Vatican II: By Those Who Were There*, ed. Alberic Stacpoole (London: Chapman, 1986), 129–52.

12. Anabaptist theologian John Howard Yoder argued that it is a mistake to focus on Constantine's reign and the Edict of Milan as the point of change. Instead, the systematic changes, such as Christians' believing that God favored the empire against its enemies, were in process long before he came along. According to Yoder, "Some of the systematic changes that Constantine as a mythic figure symbolizes for the historian (such as Christians' believing that God favored the empire against its enemies) had begun before he came along, and some (like the legal prohibition of the pagan cult or the persecution of Christian dissent) took a century after him to be worked through. So when his name is used as a mythic cipher it would be a mistake to concentrate on his biography." Yoder, "Primitivism in the Radical Reformation: Strengths and Weaknesses," in *The Primitive Church in the Modern World*, ed. Richard T. Hughes (Urbana: University of Illinois Press, 1995), 81–82.

13. This is described in historical detail by Alan Kreider, "The Impatience of Constantine," in *Patient Ferment*, 245–79.

14. Willie James Jennings details how colonialism and chattel slavery became endorsed within the church via supersessionist theological developments. Jennings, *The Christian Imagination: Theology and the Origins of Race* (New Haven: Yale University Press, 2010), 26–36, 252–63.

15. The Anabaptist Radical Reformation has traditionally located the "fall of the church" to Constantine. Others, such as Catholic theologian Yves Congar, see the ascendancy of the late twelfth-century Pope Gregory VIII as the moment when the church turned toward hierarchical power. See Congar, *Power and Poverty in the Church*. See also note 11 above.

16. John Dickson, *Bullies and Saints: An Honest Look at the Good and Evil of Christian History* (Grand Rapids: Zondervan, 2021).

17. To quote Augustine specifically, "But when those who are gifted with true godliness and live good lives also know the art of governing peoples, nothing could be more fortunate for human affairs than that, by the mercy of God, they should also have power to do so. . . . At the same time, they understand how much they lack that perfection of righteousness which exists only in the fellowship of the holy angels, of which they strive to be worthy. Moreover, however much we may praise and proclaim the virtue which serves the glory of men without true godliness, it is not for one moment to be compared with even the first and least virtue of the saints who have placed their hope in the grace and mercy of the true God." Augustine, *The City of God against the Pagans* 5.19, ed. and trans. R. W. Dyson (Cambridge: Cambridge University Press, 1998), 225–26.

18. James K. A. Smith makes a version of this point over against two-kingdoms theology. See Smith, "Reforming Public Theology: Two Kingdoms, or Two Cities?," *Calvin Theological Journal* 47 (2012): 122–37.

19. Luther says, "There are two kingdoms, one the kingdom of God, the other the kingdom of the world, . . . God's kingdom is a kingdom of grace and mercy . . . but the kingdom of the world is a kingdom of wrath and severity. Now he who would confuse these two kingdoms—as our false fanatics do—. . . would put wrath into God's kingdom and love and mercy into the world's kingdom . . . and that is the same as putting the devil in heaven and God in hell." Luther, "An Open Letter on the Harsh Book against the Harsh Peasants," in *Luther's Works*, vol. 46, *The Christian in Society*, ed. Robert C. Schultz (Philadelphia: Fortress, 1967), 46:69–70.

20. For example, in *Temporal Authority*, Luther says, "The temporal government has laws which extend no further than to life and property and external affairs on earth, for God cannot and will not permit anyone but himself to rule over the soul. Therefore, where the temporal authority presumes to prescribe laws for the soul, it encroaches upon God's government and only misleads souls and destroys them." For Luther, faith can never be coerced, "for faith is a free act, to which no one can be forced. Indeed it is a work of God in the spirit, not something which outward authority should compel or create." Luther, *Temporal Authority: To What Extent Should It Be Obeyed*, in *Luther's Works*, vol. 45, *The Christian in Society II*, ed. Walther I. Brandt (St. Louis: Concordia; Philadelphia: Fortress, 1962), 105, 108.

21. The "Luther to Hitler" legend is treated at length and critically undercut by the authors of essays in *Luther and the Modern State in Germany*, ed. James D. Tracy (Kirksville, MO: Truman State University Press, 1986).

22. The great German Lutheran New Testament historian Martin Hengel details how the "new Lutheranism and liberalism of the nineteenth and twentieth centuries" limited the right hand of God's power in Christ to the individual's inner spirituality, leaving the "all-powerful secular kingdom" to do the work of social ordering. Hengel distinguished this form of Lutheranism and two kingdoms from Luther himself. Hengel, *Christ and Power*, trans. Everett R. Kalin (Philadelphia: Fortress, 1977), 70–71.

23. See Niebuhr's accusation of Luther's quietism in *The Nature and Destiny of Man*, vol. 2, *Human Destiny* (New York: Scribner's Sons, 1943), 186–94. For a careful analysis on the various interpretations of Luther's two kingdoms and on Niebuhr's criticism of Luther, see Brent W. Sockness, "Luther's Two Kingdoms Revisited: A Response to Reinhold Niebuhr's Criticism of Luther," *Journal of Religious Ethics* 20, no. 1 (1992): 93–110.

24. This is the theme and basic thesis of Niebuhr's Gifford Lectures: *The Nature and Destiny of Man*, vol. 1, *Human Nature* (New York: Scribner's Sons, 1941), esp. 190–91.

25. Reinhold Niebuhr, *Moral Man and Immoral Society: A Study in Ethics and Politics* (New York: Charles Scribner's Sons, 1932), xxiii. Niebuhr expounds upon this thesis in the entire book.

26. Reinhold Niebuhr, *An Interpretation of Christian Ethics* (Cleveland: Meridian, 1956), chap. 2 ("The Ethic of Jesus"). "The ethic of

Jesus does not deal at all with the immediate moral problem of every human life—the problem of arranging some kind of armistice between various contending factions and forces. It has nothing to say about the relativities of politics and economics, nor of the necessary balances of power which exist and must exist in even the most intimate social relationships. The absolutism and perfectionism of Jesus's love ethic sets itself uncompromisingly not only against the natural self-regarding impulses, but against the necessary prudent defenses of the self, required because of the egoism of others. It does not establish a connection with the horizontal points of a political or social ethic or with the diagonals which a prudential individual ethic draws between the moral ideal and the facts of a given situation. It has only a vertical dimension between the loving will of God and the will of man" (45).

27. On this theme, see Niebuhr, *Nature and Destiny of Man*, 2:270–79. Perhaps there are no better pages of Niebuhr's writing to read that get to the full extent to which Niebuhr complexifies the various forms of power and in the process flattens them, so that in the world, where we must all be realists, all power is coercive power, and therefore the coercive power of each person must be balanced off against that of every other. Nathan Scott describes Niebuhr's realism in these terms in the introduction to *The Legacy of Reinhold Niebuhr*, ed. Nathan A. Scott Jr. (Chicago: University of Chicago Press, 1975), xiii.

28. Niebuhr's brother, H. Richard Niebuhr, argued much the same in this regard as his brother Reinhold. In his famous book *Christ and Culture* (New York: Harper and Row, 1956), he argued that the church should inhabit a transformationist theology of engaging culture and society's problems. But in so doing, he depicts Christ as too radical in His demands for righteousness to be of true relevance for the issues of culture. He spiritualizes Christ into a principle to be taught and enforced by worldly power. John Howard Yoder made this argument in "How H. Richard Niebuhr Reasoned: A Critique of *Christ and Culture*," in *Authentic Transformation: A New Vision of Christ and Culture*, ed. Glen H. Stassen, D. M. Yeager, and John Howard Yoder (Nashville: Abingdon, 1996), 31–89. H. Richard Niebuhr spiritualizes Christ in a way that does not allow His power to be directly relevant in cultural problems. Instead Niebuhr makes Jesus into a principle to be taught, and the church into the place to teach this justice to individuals so that they can impact their culture for the goodness and righteousness

of God as revealed in Christ. But as these individuals are sent out into the world, it is worldly power they must use. Jesus is important to Niebuhr as the teacher of justice and moral transformation, but Lord of the world, working in the world with His power, He is not. Yoder says that for H. Richard Niebuhr, "we [the human actors] are the moderators in charge of balancing the process [as to what extent we give Jesus allegiance in our decisions on ethics]. . . . We still have the last word; Christ does not. Jesus is very important; Lord he is not, if 'Lord' denotes the ultimate claim." Yoder, "How H. Richard Niebuhr Reasoned," 43.

29. In the words of Stanley Hauerwas, Reinhold Niebuhr's theology of power is a "theological justification of the irrelevance of Christianity" for politics, the work of justice, and social groups. Hauerwas, *Wilderness Wanderings* (Boulder, CO: Westview, 1997), 54. I first learned to read Niebuhr through Hauerwas (and Yoder), and I remain largely influenced by and convinced of Hauerwas's reading of Niebuhr.

30. We see the pervasive influence of Niebuhr on George W. Bush and his administration's crafting of the so-called Bush Doctrine after the terrorist attacks of 9/11. As a pious, devout Christian, Bush would rely on Jesus for his daily personal devotions but trumpet US military power as that which would protect the righteous causes of freedom and dignity. An analysis of George Bush's "Bush Doctrine" as Niebuhrian is laid out by Mark R. Amstutz, "The Bush Doctrine: A Niebuhrian Assessment," *Review of Faith and International Affairs* 5, no. 4 (December 2007): 25–33. Niebuhr fed Bush's evangelical worldview, one that sequestered godly power to our souls and was not applicable to the social ills of our broken world. Barack Obama, it is well documented, was influenced in the same way by Niebuhr. Though his policies toward war and social injustice were different than Bush's, he held to the same division of powers. See R. Ward Holder and Peter B. Josephson, "Obama's Niebuhr Problem," *Church History* 82, no. 3 (September 2013): 678–87. This influence, although not overtly named, pervades the work of James Davison Hunter, *To Change the World* (Oxford: Oxford University Press, 2010), esp. chap. 7. Hunter's influence is pervasive among evangelicals. One prominent New York evangelical pastor endorsed the book (displayed on the back over), saying, "No writer or thinker has taught me as much as James Hunter has about this all-important and complex subject of how culture is changed."

31. John Howard Yoder labeled these developments as forms of Constantinianism in "Christ, the Hope of the World," in *The Original Revolution: Essays on Christian Pacifism* (Scottdale, PA: Herald, 1971), 140–76.

Chapter 4 The Lure of Christian Nationalism

1. Elizabeth Dias, "Christianity Will Have Power," *New York Times*, August 9, 2020, https://www.nytimes.com/2020/08/09/us/evangeli cals-trump-christianity.html.

2. It is an open question within the various streams of theology whether God Himself directly exercises worldly power. Martin Luther, for the most part, pictured God as directly behind the structures of power, describing these structures as "the masks of God, behind which he wants to remain concealed and do all things." "Commentary on Psalm 147," in *Luther's Works*, vol. 14, *Selected Psalms III*, ed. Jaroslav Pelikan (St. Louis: Concordia, 1958), 114–15. Others argue that although God's sovereignty reigns, He exercises that sovereignty indirectly so as to allow the worldly powers to fulfill His preservative purposes within history. A more Anabaptist-leaning interpretation of the Persian king Cyrus, for example, sees God "allowing" Cyrus to do what he would do within the sovereign purposes of God, with the result that Cyrus accomplishes God's purposes, but in an indirect way. See the following discussion in this chapter.

3. Martin Luther, *Temporal Authority: To What Extent It Should Be Obeyed*, in *Luther's Works*, vol. 45, *The Christian in Society II*, ed. Walther I. Brandt (St. Louis: Concordia; Philadelphia: Fortress, 1962), 91, 108. For an overview of Luther's sharp distinctions in this regard in his various commentaries on the Bible, see William J. Wright, *Martin Luther's Understanding of God's Two Kingdoms: A Response to the Challenge of Skepticism* (Grand Rapids: Baker Academic, 2010), 118–26.

4. Hendrik Berkhof, in his classic book *Christ and the Powers*, characterizes these institutions as "dikes with which God encircles His good creation, to keep it in His fellowship and protect it from chaos." *Christ and the Powers*, trans. John Howard Yoder (Scottdale, PA: Herald, 1962), 29.

5. Key to the issue of whether orders such as government would be necessary if there were no sin is whether one views the state and

other orders as divinely willed, prelapsarian social structures (orders of creation) or as orders of preservation instituted by God as postlapsarian social structures. For an extended discussion on the issue, see Emil Brunner, *The Divine Imperative*, trans. Olive Wyon (Philadelphia: Westminster, 1937). He critiques his contemporary Lutheran theologian Paul Althaus's view of coercive force as natural to the created order. Althaus sees "conflict of aims" as inherent to "the natural variety of the created order." For Brunner, however, "where conflict exists which will only yield to force, there is sin, and not the divine creation" (683). For Brunner, the orders of creation have inherent merit apart from sin and are therefore worthy of preserving in this life but restored to their created goodness. Brunner acknowledges that, this side of the fall, we cannot know these orders in their original created state. "We can know no other history than that which is sinful; Original Sin has left its mark on history as a whole. But in spite of this we must hold to the belief that Creation is planned for history" (625). The danger, however, is in believing we can know God's full purposes in and through creation alone this side of the fall. For the temptation is thereby encouraged to enlist the orders of creation, including the state, in the name of God's ordained purposes. To another version of this argument by Brunner (titled "Nature and Grace") his sparring partner Karl Barth wrote a definitive rebuke entitled "No!," which can be found in Emil Brunner and Karl Barth, *Natural Theology: Comprising "Nature and Grace" by Emil Brunner and the Reply "No!" by Karl Barth*, trans. Peter Fraenkel (Eugene, OR: Wipf & Stock, 2002).

6. Stephen Wolfe in *The Case for Christian Nationalism* (Moscow, ID: Canon, 2022) repeatedly affirms the distinction between the powers of the church and the civil government (104, 299–300). And yet because the government is "natural, human and universal," implying it is given via creation, it is "for the people of God" (346). The church should therefore "pray that God would raise up [a Christian prince] from among us: one who would suppress the enemies of God and elevate his people" (323).

7. This argument has been made more extensively by the Anabaptist theologian John Howard Yoder, *The Politics of Jesus: Vicit Agnus Noster* (Grand Rapids: Eerdmans, 1972), 198–202.

8. As detailed in Olga Khazan, "Why Christians Overwhelmingly Backed Trump," *Atlantic*, November 9, 2016, https://www.theatlantic

.com/health/archive/2016/11/why-women-and-christians-backed
-trump/507176.

9. Andrew Yang, "When I Ran for President, It Messed with My Head," *Politico Magazine*, October 3, 2021, https://www.politico.com /news/magazine/2021/10/03/andrew-yang-book-excerpt-campaign ing-514967.

10. John Emerich Edward Dalberg, Lord Acton, letter to Archbishop Mandell Creighton, April 5, 1887, available at https://oll.liberty fund.org/title/acton-acton-creighton-correspondence.

11. This entire section on the principalities and powers draws from the deep literature on the topic: Berkhof, *Christ and the Powers*; Walter Wink's famous trilogy, consisting of *Naming the Powers* (Philadelphia: Fortress, 1984), *Unmasking the Powers* (Philadelphia: Fortress, 1986), and *Engaging the Powers* (Philadelphia: Fortress, 1992); and Yoder, *Politics of Jesus*, chap. 8.

12. Yoder, *Politics of Jesus*, 142.

13. Wink, *Engaging the Powers*, 8.

14. Yoder, *Politics of Jesus*, 144.

15. Hendrik Berkhof talks of being in Berlin in the 1930s studying how the *Volk* took a "new grip on men" seeking comfort, stability, and order and how people became overwhelmed by the pursuit of these conditions, allowing them to become ultimate (God) in their lives. See Berkhof, *Christ and the Powers*, 32.

16. See John Nugent, *The Politics of Yahweh: John Howard Yoder, the Old Testament, and the People of God* (Eugene, OR: Cascade Books, 2011), 72–73, 198–99.

17. Stanley Hauerwas says the moral question is not whether the fetus is a human being whose life must be protected but rather "What kind of people should we be to welcome children into the world?" In reframing the question, Hauerwas is changing the focus of the moral question of abortion from how do we frame this so as to make and enforce a law via the US government to how can we be a witness to the reality of God in Christ as it impacts how we see children and the birth of children. Hauerwas, *A Community of Character* (Notre Dame, IN: University of Notre Dame Press, 1981), 198–99.

18. Stephen Wolfe, *The Case for Christian Nationalism* (Moscow, ID: Canon, 2022), 323.

19. *The Lord of the Rings: The Fellowship of the Ring*, directed by Peter Jackson (Warner Bros Pictures, 2001).

20. Brian Zahnd (@BrianZahnd), "Just as Middle-earth could not be saved," Twitter, July 11, 2022, 6:13 p.m., https://twitter.com/Bri anZahnd/status/1546618734604959745.

Chapter 5 Playing God with Worldly Power

1. Julie Roys, "Hard Times at Harvest," *World Magazine*, December 29, 2018, https://wng.org/articles/hard-times-at-harvest-1617297601.

2. Kate Shellnut, "Harvest Elders Say James MacDonald Is 'Biblically Disqualified' from Ministry," *Christianity Today*, November 5, 2019, https://www.christianitytoday.com/news/2019/november /harvest-elders-say-james-macdonald-biblically-disqualified.html; Julie Roys, "Mancow Airs Shocking Comments by James MacDonald: My Response," Roys Report, February 12, 2019, https://julieroys.com /mancow-airs-shocking-comments-james-macdonald-response.

3. For instance, professor-therapist Chuck DeGroat diagnoses narcissism in leaders and the organizations they work for. He makes the insightful observation that "ministry is a magnet for a narcissistic personality—who else would want to speak on behalf of God every week? While the vast majority of people struggle with public speaking, . . . pastors do it regularly [and] with 'divine authority.'" DeGroat, *When Narcissism Comes to Church: Healing Your Community from Emotional and Spiritual Abuse* (Downers Grove, IL: IVP Books, 2020), 19. Here he alludes to the problem of worldly power in the service of God's purposes. But DeGroat largely sticks to challenging churches and their leaders to become aware of the endemic narcissism among leaders, become aware of how it inhabits the lives of leaders and organizations, and structure organizations to make possible a pathway toward personal spiritual growth into a deeper reliance on and centering in the presence of Christ. DeGroat's book is insightful and has much to teach us about the way leaders and organizations function in abusive ways. It does not, however, address the issue of power, which, according to my thesis, drives the pervasive abuse and coercive excess of leaders in the church.

4. Andy Crouch, *Playing God: Redeeming the Gift of Power* (Downers Grove, IL: IVP Books, 2013), 9.

5. This "realism" about power is the common starting point among many evangelicals and their theology of power. Crouch, as the one-time executive editor at the evangelical flagship publication *Christianity Today*, represents one stream of intellectual evangelicalism.

6. Crouch, *Playing God*, 48.

7. This realism about power is the common starting point for many evangelicals and their theology of power. The post–WWII influence of Abraham Kuyper, and Neo-Calvinism in general, upon evangelicals is evident. This Neo-Calvinism often starts with Gen. 1–3. Genesis 1:28 is interpreted as humanity being given a mandate by God to "fill the earth," "subdue it," and have dominion over every living thing. The church therefore sends individuals out into the cultural spheres under this cultural mandate. This fosters a sense of presumption that, indeed, Christians are endowed with the mandate to exercise power to order culture to God's purposes. This is in keeping with Kuyper's famous dictum, "There is not one square inch in the whole domain of our human existence over which Christ, who is Sovereign over *all*, does not cry: 'Mine!'" James D. Bratt, ed., *Abraham Kuyper: A Centennial Reader* (Grand Rapids: Eerdmans, 1998), 461. In similar fashion, Stephen Wolfe begins his book on Christian nationalism with an exegesis of Gen. 1:26–28. Wolfe, *The Case for Christian Nationalism* (Moscow, ID: Canon, 2022), 21–22. The temptation to use "power over" in the name of God often starts with Gen. 1:26–20.

8. Crouch, *Playing God*, 33.

9. Crouch's caricature of evangelicals and Genesis has itself become a trope among evangelicals. Evangelicals, the trope goes, start with Gen. 3, missing entirely Gen. 1 and 2, where creation is created as good. Evangelicals emphasize sin and forget the goodness of God's creation. Crouch tips his hat to this trope when he says, "Many evangelical tellings of the biblical story . . . effectively begin with Genesis 3: the fall of humanity. . . . The original good creation and the glorious new creation are afterthoughts when they are mentioned at all." Crouch, *Playing God*, 30.

10. Crouch, *Playing God*, 162–64.

11. Crouch, *Playing God*, 170–75.

12. Crouch, *Playing God*, 220.

13. Crouch, *Playing God*, 237–40.

14. For authors who recognize the potential for Christian practices to be used in ways that are corrupting, see James K. A. Smith, *Awaiting the King: Reforming Public Theology* (Grand Rapids: Baker Academic, 2017), chap. 6; Lauren F. Winner, *The Dangers of Christian Practice: On Wayward Gifts, Characteristic Damage, and Sin* (New Haven: Yale University Press, 2018). Neither, however, locates

the problem with practices in the problem of power. A practice works in the Christian faith when it disciplines you to come "under the power" of God and His presence. This is the act of faith. This is what makes possible participation in a sacrament.

15. Diane Langberg, *Redeeming Power: Understanding Authority and Abuse in the Church* (Grand Rapids: Brazos, 2020), 3.

16. Langberg, *Redeeming Power*, 4.

17. Langberg, *Redeeming Power*, 6.

18. Langberg, *Redeeming Power*, 13.

19. Langberg, *Redeeming Power*, 16.

20. Langberg, *Redeeming Power*, 31–33.

21. Langberg, *Redeeming Power*, 42.

22. Langberg, *Redeeming Power*, 53.

23. Langberg, *Redeeming Power*, 79–83.

24. Langberg, *Redeeming Power*, 89.

25. Langberg, *Redeeming Power*, chap. 8.

26. Langberg, *Redeeming Power*, chaps. 11–12. An example of how she calls persons to exercise power differently but keeps the "power over" in place is seen where she says, "Pastors and elders have authority over sheep. Husbands and wives have power over each other." But authority must "be exercised in love or else it is no authority at all. . . . In the end the bridge is there . . . that allows for the power to corrupt . . . and do it in the name of better character" (178–79).

27. Dominique DuBois Gilliard, *Subversive Witness: Scripture's Call to Leverage Privilege* (Grand Rapids: Zondervan, 2021), xxiii.

28. Gilliard, *Subversive Witness*, 6–7.

29. Gilliard, *Subversive Witness*, 8–9.

30. Gilliard, *Subversive Witness*, xxiii–xxiv.

31. Gilliard, *Subversive Witness*, xxiii–xxiv.

32. Gilliard spends whole chapters on these tactics.

33. Peggy McIntosh, "White Privilege and Male Privilege: A Personal Account of Coming to See Correspondences through Work in Women's Studies," in *Privilege: A Reader*, ed. Michael S. Kimmel and Abby L. Ferber (Boulder, CO: Westview, 2014), 23–24.

34. Gilliard, *Subversive Witness*, chap. 7.

35. Although it does appear that a certain class of robbers who were not part of any system of monetary exchange were required to pay fourfold. See, for instance, I. Howard Marshall, *The Gospel of Luke: A Commentary on the Greek Text* (Grand Rapids: Zondervan, 1978), 698.

36. Most notably, Walter Brueggemann argues that Joseph isn't included when God is named as "God of X" (of Abraham, Isaac, Jacob) in the Old Testament because Joseph is a "sellout." His aligning with Egyptian power is what led to his people's induction into Egyptian slavery. Brueggemann, "A Fourth-Generation Sellout," in *The Collected Sermons of Walter Brueggemann* (Louisville: Westminster John Knox, 2011), 164–68.

37. On Cyrus in this regard, see John Nugent, *The Politics of Yahweh: John Howard Yoder, the Old Testament, and the People of God* (Eugene, OR: Cascade Books, 2011), 72–73, 198–99. On how Joseph went against God's ways of land organization for the flourishing of all people and instead enslaved his people, see this insightful Twitter thread by New Testament scholar and professor Andrew Rillera (@AndrewRillera), "Y'all know I'm a big fan of," Twitter, June 29, 2023, 5:07 p.m., https://twitter.com/AndrewRillera/status/1674525078040756224.

38. Brian Klaas, *Corruptible: Who Gets Power and How It Changes Us* (New York: Scribner, 2021), 41.

39. Klaas, *Corruptible*, 37–59.

Chapter 6 Living under the Power of Christ

1. Saul Alinsky describes a view of reconciliation caught in the frame that somebody must win and the other person must lose. It is the way of worldly power. "We live in a world where 'reconciliation' means that when one side gets the power, the other side gets reconciled to it." Alinsky, *Rules for Radicals: A Practical Primer for Realistic Radicals* (New York: Vintage, 1989), 13. I contend that central to Jesus's practice of reconciliation is that both sides give up worldly power and submit to the authority of Christ.

2. Markus Barth argues that we should not shy away from translating *phobos* in Eph. 5:21 as "fear," as opposed to a weaker notion of "respect" or "reverence." The fear of God is not about a fear of retribution or violent punishment. Rather, this fear is about being in the very presence of the awesome, powerful, and good God. It is much like the *phobos* experienced by the disciples as they encountered the miraculous deeds and words of Jesus (Mark 4:41; 5:15, 33; 6:6; 16:8). It has to do with the numinous encounter of God's presence in the temple. And so we see here that mutual submission is made possible by a profound encounter with the lordship of Jesus at work

in the midst of our lives. See Barth, *Ephesians 4–6*, Anchor Bible 34A (Garden City, NY: Doubleday, 1974), 662–68, esp. 664–65.

3. I have often sought after a word to replace "submission." The best replacement is "yieldedness," a word suggested by my friend David Boshart. See Boshart, "Yieldedness Is the Way Forward," *The Mennonite* (April 2016).

4. This paragraph assumes the fivefold giftings of church leadership as displayed in Eph. 4:11–12, where "apostle" is an ongoing gift. I follow those who observe that the word "apostle" is used in the New Testament to refer beyond the original Twelve and Paul. See Acts 14:4; Rom. 16:7; 2 Cor. 8:23; Phil. 2:25; 1 Thess. 1:1; 2:7.

5. The German Mennonite tradition uses the word *gelassenheit* to describe the experience of being together in this space. There is much to be learned from the cultivation of *gelassenheit* within the Mennonite tradition. See Don Clymer, "Gelassenheit: A Spiritual Journey," *Mennonite World Review* (June 23, 2017): 14. Thanks to David Boshart for reminding me of this great tradition of the Mennonites.

6. I am convinced that Paul is addressing a group of individuals, under the influence of Gnosticism, who are overstepping their authority, pridefully claiming their authority based on speaking in tongues. Paul refers to these people as "the spiritual ones." This translation of *pneumatikoi* is not scholarly consensus. See W. J. Bartling, "The Congregation of Christ and Charismatic Body," *Concordia Theological Monthly* 40 (1969): 68–70; Ulrich Wilckens, "Sophia," in *Theological Dictionary of the New Testament* (Grand Rapids: Eerdmans, 1971), 7:519–22. See the discussion in Gordon D. Fee, *The First Epistle to the Corinthians* (Grand Rapids: Eerdmans, 1987), 575–76.

7. Timothy G. Gombis details how the apostle Paul rids himself of hierarchy and posture over people in his leadership among the churches. Gombis, *Power in Weakness: Paul's Transformed Vision for Ministry* (Grand Rapids: Eerdmans, 2021), 108–13, 145–47.

8. John Piper and Wayne Grudem, eds., *Recovering Biblical Manhood and Womanhood: A Response to Evangelical Feminism* (Wheaton: Crossway, 1991).

9. One way to read 1 Tim. 2:11–12 is that Paul is exhorting women to mutually submit and to reject usurping "power over" when they teach. They are to reject "power over" in general wherever it may be, including when they exercise their newfound authority in their teaching gifts.

10. There's significant historical evidence that substantiates that women's emergence as leaders in the first centuries of the church happened from the bottom up, in small house gatherings, as opposed to leadership through ecclesiastical structures. It was through godly power, unleashed in the Spirit among a people, where women first thrived as leaders versus the "power over" ecclesiastical structures that emerged in the post-Constantinian period. See Carolyn Osiek and Margaret Y. MacDonald, *A Woman's Place: House Churches in Earliest Christianity* (Minneapolis: Fortress, 2006).

11. For a review of how the three spaces—"temples," homes, and other social spaces—work throughout the New Testament, see David E. Fitch, *Faithful Presence: Seven Disciplines That Shape the Church for Mission* (Downers Grove, IL: IVP Books, 2016); Fitch, *What Is the Church and Why Does It Exist?* (Harrisonburg, VA: Herald, 2021) chaps. 5, 6.

12. Korie L. Edwards, *The Elusive Dream: The Power of Race in Interracial Churches* (New York: Oxford University Press, 2008), 126.

13. For a full-length treatment of how ideology works in our churches, see David Fitch, *The Church of Us vs. Them* (Grand Rapids: Brazos, 2019).

14. See Craig Hovey, "Free Christian Speech: Plundering Foucault," *Political Theology* 8, no. 1 (2007): 63–81.

15. These lectures can be found in Michel Foucault, *"Discourse & Truth" and "Parrēsia,"* ed. Henri-Paul Fruchaud and Daniele Lorenzine (Chicago: University of Chicago Press, 2019). For a helpful summary of Foucault's work on *parrhēsia*, see Tina Besley and Michael A. Peters, *Subjectivity and Truth: Foucault, Education, and the Culture of Self* (New York: Peter Lang, 2007), chap. 5.

16. Martin Luther King Jr. famously made his case for embodied presence from his prison cell in Birmingham in 1963. He wrote, "We had no alternative except that of preparing for direct action, whereby we would present our very bodies as a means of laying our case before the conscience of the local and national community." For King, the idea of bodily, face-to-face "presence" had the goal of creating a "constructive non-violent tension" in the minds of the public versus a "violent tension." King, "Letter from Birmingham Jail," April 16, 1963, published as "The Negro Is Your Brother," *Atlantic Monthly* 212, no. 2 (August 1963): 78–88. This constructive nonviolent tension is presence. When inhabited by Christ, it disrupts the powers. It upends

worldly power. It is dangerous. Christ was crucified and King was assassinated in this tension. But thus is the beginning of true reconciliation and transformation.

17. Oscar Romero, *The Violence of Love*, trans. James R. Brockman (Maryknoll, NY: Orbis Books, 2004), x.

Epilogue

1. See Harry Bruinius, "Millennial Evangelicals Push for Full Inclusion of LGBT Christians," *Christian Science Monitor*, February 20, 2015, https://www.csmonitor.com/USA/2015/0220/Millennial -Evangelicals-push-for-full-inclusion-of-LGBT-Christians. Bruinius reports on Pew Foundation polls, David Gushee's presentation at "The Reformation Project Conference" in Washington, DC, and other evidences of the millennial surge of support for LGBTQ inclusion among evangelicals. In all cases the argument was used that the church has been on the wrong side of history so many times, especially regarding slavery and women's rights, that we must revise our view of same-sex sexuality before we fail once again.

2. See David A. Graham, "The Wrong Side of 'the Right Side of History,'" *Atlantic*, December 21, 2015, https://www.theatlantic.com /politics/archive/2015/12/obama-right-side-of-history/420462.

3. Martin Luther King Jr. often used the phrase "the arc of history bends toward justice" in speeches, most famously in a speech entitled "Remaining Awake through a Great Revolution" delivered at the National Cathedral on March 31, 1968. For an earlier version of that speech, see King, "Remaining Awake through a Great Revolution," Oberlin College commencement address, June 1965, Oberlin, Ohio, https://www2.oberlin.edu/external/EOG/BlackHistoryMonth /MLK/CommAddress.html.

4. Walter Rauschenbusch saw democracy as the manifestation of God's kingdom. See Rauschenbusch, *A Theology for the Social Gospel* (New York: Abingdon, 1917), 111–13.

5. Reinhard Hutter describes Rauschenbusch's conception of history as "historicist immanentism" in "The Church: Midwife of History or Witness to the Eschaton?," *Journal of Religious Ethics* 18 (1990): 27–54. This view of history presumes that God is at work guiding history within this closed system and nothing can stop its progress.

6. Oxford historian Herbert Butterfield outlines how the "right side of history" argument could be used by those in power to seize the

(contrived) moral high ground. In the preface of *The Whig Interpretation of History* (1931; repr., New York: Norton, 1965), he says the tendency with many historians is "to write on the side of Protestants and Whigs, to praise revolutions provided they have been successful, to emphasize certain principles of progress in the past and to produce a story which is the ratification if not the glorification of the present" (v).

7. Jemar Tisby, *The Color of Compromise: The Truth about the American Church's Complicity in Racism* (Grand Rapids: Zondervan, 2019), 17.

8. Tisby, *Color of Compromise*, 48.

9. Tisby, *Color of Compromise*, 50–51.

10. Tisby details these splits in *Color of Compromise*, 76–77.

11. Tisby, *Color of Compromise*, chap. 9.

12. Donald W. Dayton, *Rediscovering an Evangelical Heritage: A Tradition and Trajectory of Integrating Piety and Justice* (Grand Rapids: Baker Academic, 2014), chap. 1.

13. Donald Dayton details how these New School Presbyterians were the Methodistic party of Presbyterianism. The "new measures" ("protracted meetings," the use of women, the "anxious bench," extemporaneous prayer and preaching, etc.) of Finney's revivalism were largely drawn from Methodist practices. Dayton, "The Search for the Historical Evangelicalism: George Marsden's History of Fuller Seminary as a Case Study," *Christian Scholar's Review* 23, no. 1 (1993): 16, 32.

14. An important book in this regard is Robert L. Allen, *Reluctant Reformers: Racism and Social Reform Movements in the United States* (Washington, DC: Howard University Press, 1974). Allen explores the mixed motives among abolitionists, participants in women's rights movements, and other social reformers. Dayton, in conversations before his passing, told me of his many conversations with Robert Allen on this subject. Dayton's comments on the failure of the early abolitionist movements to completely reject racism can be found in Donald W. Dayton, "Piety and Radicalism: Ante-Bellum Social Evangelicalism in the U.S.," in *From the Margins: A Celebration of the Theological Work of Donald W. Dayton*, ed. Christian T. Collins Winn (Eugene, OR: Pickwick, 2007), 34–36.

15. Dayton, *Rediscovering an Evangelical Heritage*, 179–80.

16. Dayton plays on this theme in numerous scholarly articles as well as in his books. See Christian T. Collins Winn's analysis of Dayton's take on this in his introduction to *From the Margins*, xx–xxi.

17. Dayton, *Rediscovering an Evangelical Heritage*, 169.

18. Ada María Isasi-Díaz, "Mujeristas: A Name of Our Own," *Christian Century*, May 24–31, 1989, 560. See, from the Latin American perspective, Jon Sobrino, *No Salvation outside the Poor: Prophetic-Utopian Essays* (Maryknoll, NY: Orbis Books, 2008), chap. 2. Carter Heyward says this is not "a romanticization of the poor's capacity to know what is right or wrong, any more than other folks do. The epistemological privilege of the poor is, rather, the *ability* (or 'privilege') to know first and best what it is—to experience the call and push of God against poverty, against the economic system and social structures that generate poverty, and against the greed and ignorance and stupidity that hold poverty in place. The epistemological privilege of the poor also puts a moral and political mandate before the non-poor—that is, the rest of us—to listen to the poor; to take seriously what we hear and see and learn; and to act in solidarity with the poor in the struggles for bread and justice." Heyward, *Saving Jesus from Those Who Are Right: Rethinking What It Means to Be Christian* (Minneapolis: Fortress, 1999), 224n4.

19. James Cone, *God of the Oppressed*, rev. ed. (Maryknoll, NY: Orbis Books, 1997), 31.

20. James Cone, *The Cross and the Lynching Tree* (Maryknoll, NY, Orbis Books, 2011), 154. See also Cone's extended conversation on Martin Luther King Jr. and redemptive suffering via God's work in the suffering (83–92).

21. Most notably, Cone is scathing in his rebuke of his colleague Reinhold Niebuhr's distance from the actual suffering of the African American. Cone tells us how Niebuhr could talk about the plight of the Black person in America—including giving a brutal assessment of White privilege in America—and then, on the other hand, disappointingly speak with a dispassionate, calculating approach about patiently accommodating the evil and solving the problem over time. Cone in essence is describing Niebuhr's lack of a posture, and presence, among the poor. Cone asks, Why the contradiction between Niebuhr's intellectual positions and the way he actually lived them out? Cone answered by saying that Niebuhr failed "to step into black people's shoes and 'walk around in them.' . . . It was easy for Niebuhr to walk around in his own shoes, as a white man, and view the world from that vantage point, but it takes a whole lot of empathic effort to step into those of black people and see the world through the eyes

of African Americans." Cone, *The Cross and the Lynching Tree*, 40. Though influenced by Reinhold Niebuhr, Martin Luther King Jr. found Niebuhr's Christology insufficient to the task of leading a nonviolent, disruptive presence in Montgomery and beyond. See an account of King's critique of Niebuhr in Charles Marsh, *The Beloved Community: How Faith Shapes Social Justice, from the Civil Rights Movement to Today* (New York: Basic Books, 2005), 39–41.

22. Andrew Marin, *Us versus Us: The Untold Story of Religion and the LGBT Community* (Colorado Springs: NavPress, 2016), xix.

23. Marin, *Us versus Us*, 38, 54.

24. Marin, *Us versus Us*, 35.

25. There are many resources on this. I recommend starting with historian Alan Kreider's *The Patient Ferment of the Early Church: The Improbable Rise of Christianity in the Roman Empire* (Grand Rapids: Baker Academic, 2016).

26. The impact and Christian roots of the SNCC movement are charted by Marsh, *Beloved Community*, 87–126.

27. These events are recounted in William T. Cavanaugh, *Torture and Eucharist: Theology, Politics, and the Body of Christ* (Oxford: Blackwell, 1998).

28. Emmanuel Katongole tells these stories in his *The Journey of Reconciliation: Groaning for New Creation in Africa* (Maryknoll, NY: Orbis Books, 2017). This is just one of his many marvelous theological engagements with Christianity, Africa, and the witness of reconciliation.